Free-Heel Skiing

The Secrets of Telemark and Parallel Techniques—In All Conditions

FREE-HEEL SKIING

The Secrets of Telemark and Parallel Techniques—In All Conditions

Paul Parker

Chelsea Green Publishing Company
Chelsea, Vermont

Diadem Books, Ltd. · London

Published in Britain by Diadem Books, Ltd.
All trade enquiries U.K. and Commonwealth to
Cordee, 3a DeMontfort St.,
Leicester LE1 7HD, England
ISBN 0-906371-67-8 (UK)

Library of Congress Cataloging-in-Publication Data

Parker, Paul, 1953-
    Free-heel skiing.

    Includes index.
    1. Telemark (Skiing)   2. Telemark (Skiing) — History.
I. Title
GV854.9.T44P37   1988   796.93   88-18966
ISBN 0-930031-18-0 (alk. paper)

Thanks, Vincent

ACKNOWLEDGMENTS & CREDITS

Yvon Chouinard, Kris McDivitt, Lito Tejada-Flores, Michael Kennedy, Steve McDonald, Members of the PSIA Alpine Demonstration Team, and especially all my infamous teammates on the PSIA Nordic Demonstration Team made this book possible.

Illustrations
Steve McDonald

Photography
Michael Kennedy
Ace Kvale
John Laptad
John Moynier
Larry Proser
Satoshi Ishizu

Part Opening Photographs
1 John Falkiner in Verbier, Switzerland
   Photo by Ace Kvale

2 Free-heel jump turns in Verbier
   Photo by Ace Kvale

3 Off piste
   Photo by Ace Kvale

4 The author off piste near Sapporro, Japan
   Photo by Yaraicho Skinjuko-ku

CONTENTS

2 BASIC TECHNIQUES: YOUR FOUNDATION

3 ADVANCED FREE-HEEL TECHNIQUES

4 FREE-HEELING IN POWDER, CRUD, AND MOGULS

FOREWORD

Until I started watching and listening to Paul Parker, I had taught myself to ski by just going out and doing it. I have short, strong legs and had done enough backcountry skiing to get pretty good at survival turns.

I was introduced to cross-country skis and the telemark turn about twelve years ago by Doug Robinson and his band of "Armadillos" on the east side of the Sierra. At the time, I couldn't understand why they insisted on messing with the pine tar and klister and zigzagging around instead of simply slapping on some skins and going straight up the hill. And those weird drop-knee turns! Why not just parallel or do survival stem christies?

A few years later I found myself coming down Denali pulling a fifty-pound sled through eighteen inches of heavy new snow. I put the load on my back, thinking I could easily ski this stuff on my alpine touring skis, but soon realized that with the load, the wet snow, and the floppy mountain boots there was no way I could begin to initiate a turn. So I unlatched my heels and headed down with a sort of snowplow/stem/telemark/steering turn. No unweighting was necessary or possible. This experience was a revelation to me and soon afterwards I hung up my fat boards and went skinny.

Corn was the new diet. A typical morning in May or June would find me hiking up some slope in the Tetons or Absarokas, maybe sitting on top for an hour or so to let the corn become velvet, then cutting down in wide, classic telemarks.

But it was while skiing with Artie Burrows, Julie Neils, and Murray Cunningham in Aspen that my eyes were first opened to the full potential of skinny skis. Not only were these people outskiing nearly

The author and Yvon Chouinard
after an especially good run
at Niseko, Hokkaido, Japan
Photo by Satoshi Ishizu

everyone on the mountain regardless of gear, but theirs was not the Peruvian-hat, double-poling, Al Jolson-mammy-turn technique I had known. These jaded ex-alpine racers were blending the old with the new to create an entirely original sport. I was stoked, but I had some work to do! This is about the time I started to really watch and listen to Paul Parker.

Paul is my kind of instructor. He gives me a one-sentence technique tip, then leaves me alone until he sees that I've digested it. I have been given more than a few tips by him over the years while skiing *toute neige-toute terrain* in various off-beat parts of the world, as we've traveled together testing equipment.

There was a day in Steamboat, skiing hardpack, paralleling the steep stuff, and telemarking the intermediate hills. I'd always had trouble with my left-hand teles and Paul told me to think about pressing the little toe of my back foot against the slope. This worked to get my feet closer together and my skis on edge and corrected my habit of going into my left turns from a stem.

A few days later, a foot of heavy, skied-out cement in Breckenridge stopped me cold. Paul told me to exaggerate my ups and downs the way skiers used to do before high-top plastic boots. This worked, too.

In Hokkaido we met up with fifteen members of the 200-member Japanese Telemark Association. None of them had skied outside Japan, and they were anxious to watch Parker to see if they were on the right track. They were all excellent skiers on the pistes, skiing in perfect Austrian feet-locked-together style. No yelling, and no smiling. When it snowed a meter we headed for the trees—all birch and giant bamboo—and Paul gave me a powder tip. He told me to pretend to grip a pencil between my hip and waist. This got my skis off to the side and together. Switching from side to side got the powder rhythm going and I made five or six good turns before I blew it. Not bad, though. Nor were the Japanese much better in the powder. I sensed them wondering why we didn't just go back to those nicely packed slopes.

The next day Paul told me not to let my hand drop down and back. As soon as I planted my pole, the other hand came forward. "Let out a big, aggressive grunt every time you do a turn," he said. I did this and suddenly it all came together—we were like two hooting kamikazes, grunting and screaming through the trees, finally breaking out of the woods and laughing our heads off, covered from head to toe in the white stuff. Very un-Japanese.

I can't always listen to Parker. Sometimes I have to just watch. A few years ago several of us spent a week in the Sierra skiing the peaks north of Mount Whitney. It was late spring and there had been a day of wet snow and rain followed by a couple of cold nights, so when going out over Shepherd Pass it was no surprise to find the north side a sheet of ice. No way was I going to even attempt traverses or kick turns on that thirty-five degrees of smooth ice. I climbed down the rocks, paralleling the gully as far as I could, and was searching through my pack for something sharp and hard to scratch steps, when I looked up to see Parker with his forty-pound pack jump-turning down in perfect control. We all watched fairly aghast, when Paul stopped, looked down at his feet, and calmly announced that the bail on one of his experimental bindings had broken on one side. He pushed off again, this time being careful to keep the one ski on the ice so he didn't jump out of the binding. By the time he was safely down I was so shattered that I threw off my heavy pack and watched it whirl down in great leaps for hundreds of feet to the snowfield below. Then I pulled out a couple of tent pegs and started scratching nicks in the ice, lowering myself down on my belly.

"Hey, Paul. Wait for me."

Yvon Chouinard

IT'S ALL SKIING

Downhill skiing on skinny skis can be like driving a '55 Ford with bald tires—skiddy, unsure, and imprecise. Alpine skiing is at the other end of the spectrum: fast, crisp, and exact—more like driving a Porsche. My goal in both skiing and teaching the sport has been to combine these two extremes in a marriage of free-heel mobility with Alpine precision. It works.

I was a member of the Professional Ski Instructors of America Nordic Demonstration Team for eight years, so much of my teaching has been Nordic, both in track and in free-heel slope techniques. But the experience that has contributed the most to my free-heel/Alpine "marriage" has been gained from teaching Alpine skiing. The opportunity to study Alpine ideas and apply them to my skinnier skis has been invaluable. And that is the purpose of this book: to present *all* of the techniques available to the free-heel skier, not just telemark technique. The final goal is to give you more technical ammo for tackling challenging terrain and snow.

Each winter I set a goal for my skiing. That goal might be skiing a certain tour, a special race, or descending a peak or couloir I've been eyeing. Often my goal has been technique related—learning a new one, perfecting an old one, or ridding myself of a bad one. Of course, there's room for more than one goal, as long as I can see them all the way through. Goals keep me interested. They give me something to look forward to through the winter, and they give me something to work for.

I want you to set a goal for this book, one that you would like to achieve with your reading and practice. A goal will increase your curiosity and your interest in learning. Are you a novice free-heel skier—do you want to learn basic turns? Do you want to learn a new technique or an alternative to one you are using now? Are you looking for a breakthrough — do you feel like a terminal intermediate? Maybe you'd like to learn to ski those "other" conditions — powder, crud, moguls? Or do you simply want more control of your Nordic skis or more fun on the trail when faced with a downhill?

Throughout this book I've used the term "free-heel" with skis, skiers, and skiing. Free-heel is an inclusive word that also points to the most essential difference between skiers who use Alpine and skiers who use Nordic equipment. Backcountry, cross-country, and telemark skiers and equipment are *free-heel*. This book is written for those skiers, whether they're at the beginner, intermediate, or expert level, to satisfy their goals.

You can start with the section that best fits your needs and abilities. If you are a beginner you might begin your reading with "Basic Techniques." You might want to learn telemark only, but read about Alpine techniques, too. They will improve your telemark skiing as well as your understanding of what your skis are doing.

If your skiing is more advanced, skip "Basic Techniques" and go right to "Advanced Free-heel Techniques" — but go back later and read about the basics. These techniques form your foundation and are important for even the most advanced skier. And, advanced skiers, pay heed to the technical nuances of the turns described in Part IV, "Free-heeling in Powder, Crud, and Moguls." More than any style of skier, advanced telemarkers tend to be muscle and survival skiers, skiing more on guts and less on technique. Take advantage of those "Alpine" ideas — you won't believe what you can do with them. But in the end, it doesn't matter where the ideas come from. It's all skiing.

Paul Parker

Free-Heel Skiing

The Secrets of Telemark and Parallel Techniques—In All Conditions

1
BEGINNINGS

FREE-HEEL ROOTS

The real fathers of the sport were not the men who made a few half-hearted experiments with skis and then abandoned the fickle boards in despair, but those who first proved by solid achievement the wonderful possibilities of the ski.
— Arnold Lunn

Throughout modern ski history one theme recurs—that of the gradual development of two separate skiing disciplines—Alpine and Nordic. Early masters of the two schools fought like rival siblings to establish theirs as the superior one. Yet neither style succumbed. Instead, each grew more specialized for its home terrain. Alpine remained purely downhill technique. It was the Nordic skier who preserved the option to ski either up *or* down.

The "rebirth" of the telemark has brought these two rivals back onto the same terrain. Yet there is still a distance that separates the two, one that, fortunately for the sport of skiing, is shrinking. What today is only a technical or aesthetic difference began as a heartfelt rivalry a hundred years ago.

The feud between Nordic and Alpine came late in the sport's development, once ski technique had matured. Long before that, skiing's earliest beginnings originated in the far north. Most historians credit Scandinavia with the birth of skiing, but some believe it was introduced in China, not for traveling across snow but for support on peat bogs and mud flats while collecting duck eggs.

Arnold Lunn supports this theory. "Pattens have been employed from time immemorial not only on snow, but for crossing mud, sand, lava. . . ." For most, the start of skiing was on snow in Scandinavia. Numerous archeological discoveries in Norway, Sweden, and Lapland substantiate this theory.

Early skis varied in length and shape and were made from ash, pine, or birch. Some were solid boards with the tips soaked or steamed and turned up. Others were frames of wood covered in leather. Skiers used one long pole which they dragged as a brake and used as an outrigger. While many skis in the far north were short and wide, Lapland skis were of varying lengths. The shorter ski had a kind of "climbing skin" made from fur for uphill purchase; the longer ski was used for glide. Farther south, skis were long and of equal length and resembled skis used in the 1930s.

THE NORWEGIAN TECHNIQUE

Sondre Norheim is considered the father of Norwegian technique. It was Norheim who, in the late 1800s, developed the telemark on the slopes around his town of Morgedal in Telemark, Norway. He introduced the telemark to the world at a jumping competition in Oslo in 1868, where he not only awed a large crowd with his seventy-six-foot jump but also punctuated his landing with a graceful telemark turn to a stop.

The telemark turn wasn't just a curiosity but a viable technique for the equipment of the day, which consisted of free heels and wood skis with no side-cut. In the telemark position one

Wood-laminated Alpine skis circa 1940
Nanni Tua Collection

could wedge the forward ski slightly and have the effect of one long, side-cut ski. When properly performed the result was an elegant arc, most often a medium-to-long radius turn well suited to Norway's moderate terrain and deep snow.

Another significant contributor to this Norwegian school was the explorer Fridthjof Nansen. In 1888 Nansen completed a 500-kilometer journey across southern Greenland and in 1890 published a book about the expedition, *The First Crossing of Greenland.* It was the first widely read account of ski technique, development, and philosophy.

Inspired by the California Gold Rush, the Norwegians opened a branch for their school in America. Many emigrating Norwegians stopped en route to California and settled in the Midwest, but one, John A. Thorenson, made it all the way to California. Thorenson was later nicknamed "Snowshoe" Thompson for the mail route he pioneered over the formidable Sierra Nevada. For twenty years he carried mail from California to the Nevada mining camps. The combined weight of his oak skis and the mail on his back sometimes exceeded one hundred pounds.

THE ALPINE TECHNIQUE

Although later bolstered by nationalistic pride, the split between Alpine and Nordic skiing did have technical roots. The Alpine countries of Central Europe depended on ski troops for the defense of their mountainous borders. Yet negotiating the Alps required a different style of skiing with its steep, unforgiving couloirs and rock-strewn slopes. The Alpine school evolved using braking techniques with smaller, more controlled turns.

The Austrian Mathias Zdarsky is most often credited as the "father" of Alpine technique. In his book *Lilienfelder skilauf technik* Zdarsky documented the snowplow turn he performed on his short, compact skis.

Father or not, it sounds like Zdarsky must have been a real ass. He vehemently promoted the rift between the Alpine and Nordic schools and directed personal, vindictive abuse against his colleagues using Norwegian technique in the nearby Black Forest. In retrospect it is amusing. Historian Arnold Lunn referred to the infamous feud as the "Battle of the Bindings."

The bindings *were* different, but unlike today, both Alpine and Nordic bindings were free-heeled. The early Nordic bindings resembled today's cable bindings in that they hinged farther back, under the ball of the foot. The Alpine bindings, however, hinged in front of the toe like a modern randonnée binding. It's no wonder that Zdarsky didn't like telemark turns—anyone who has tried to telemark on randonnée gear knows the desperate insecurity of tiptoeing on the rear foot.

Zdarsky skied with only one long pole. It was Georg Bilgeri, an Austrian colonel, who popularized the use of two shorter poles. Bilgeri checked his speed with his turns rather than with an outrigger. He published his techniques, but didn't follow any particular "school" of skiing. Bilgeri suggested that Alpine skiers use the strong points of both the Norwegian and Alpine schools, describing the "stembogen," or stem turn—a snowplow turn linked by a diagonal run—inspired by the snowplow and telemark.

Zdarsky suffered sour grapes over any notoriety that Bilgeri might have enjoyed. He was so angered by Bilgeri's description of the stembogen in his book *Der Alpin Skilauf* that he challenged the colonel to a duel. Had the duel been carried out, and had Bilgeri been a good shot, the modern relationship between Nordic and Alpine might be much different. But it wasn't only Zdarsky who decided the split between the two techniques. Part of the handiwork belonged to Rudolph Lettner, an Austrian metal worker who put metal edges on his skis to keep them from splintering. Not only did the edges increase the life of his skis but they gave his turns more carve and less skid.

The so-called "Arlberg technique" developed by using more commitment, more angles of the body. The Arlberg skier stood far forward with his upper body rotated. His turns were initiated with a stem. Hannes Schneider, a student of Bilgeri's, was responsible for developing the Arlberg as a system for Alpine instruction. He combined telemark and stembogen into his Arlberg turn, an early version of the stem christy. He presented his progression of skills to ski schools in 1912, and it dominated downhill ski instruction worldwide until the 1940s.

Telemark was officially dead, at least for Alpine instruction. The techniques split—Arlberg for downhill skiing, telemark for tourers in up-and-down terrain.

POST-WAR DEVELOPMENTS

The Second World War brought skiing as a sport to a standstill. Ironically, for Americans the war set the stage for skiing's future. Since fighting in the mountains of Europe necessitated skiing and mountaineering skills, Minot "Minnie" Dole—who later founded the National Ski Patrol—formed the 87th Mountain Infantry Division. The 87th was soon re-named as it is better known today: the Tenth Mountain Division. After the war surviving veterans of the Tenth Mountain Division returned to start the ski areas, ski schools, ski shops, and ski-manufacturing companies that have turned the sport of American skiing into a viable industry.

Nordic skiing did not see as much development, but Alpine grew rapidly. In 1946, the first ski-snowshoe race was held at Arapahoe Basin in Colorado. First prize was a can of beer. In 1950, Aspen hosted a World-Cup race. In that same year, Cubco bindings were introduced. Their spring-loaded heel piece held the ski-boot heel securely on the ski. This specialization in equipment set the modern course for Alpine skiing as the lift-serviced sport that we know it as today. Free-heeled bindings remained popular with off-piste skiers and ski mountaineers, but for lift-serviced Alpine skiers Cubcos became state-of-the-art.

As Alpine skiing grew, many more ski lifts were built. Downhill skiers, confined to a similar path down resort slopes, soon formed moguls. The Arlberg became a dated technique. Its slow, elegant, exaggerated movements were incompatible with the bump-studded hills. Alpine turns became quicker.

In 1959, Cliff Taylor developed his Graduated Length Method, a mixed blessing in the development of skiing.

Admittedly, it did allow more people to more easily learn the sport, but what had once been nice, round moguls developed into evil little ski-bending bumps. With GLM's development many Alpine skiers, disgusted by hackers' short skis ruining even the steepest slopes, ventured into the backcountry.

In the early 1970s, in Crested Butte, Colorado, and a number of little backcountry pockets around the snowy U.S., skiers exhumed the telemark, a technique that brought downhill stability to their free-heeled gear. They could tour off the Alpine trails and make sweeping turns in idyllic snow inaccessible to the short Alpine skis. They could get back to the sport's beginnings, where many of them thought it should stay.

The telemark turn was reborn.

An important contributor to telemark's rebirth is Rick Borkovek. A long-time resident of Crested Butte, Rick published a number of articles on the tele's comeback that inspired mountaineers and ski tourers to give it a try. Manufacturers were urged to make new products for telemarkers. First, plastic-laminated cross-country skis were developed with aluminum edges. These evolved into "skinny Alpine skis" with tunable steel edges. As

skis got wider boots got higher and stiffer, first home-modified by the hardcore piste skiers then factory-made as the demand for them grew.

In the mid-1970s, the competitive urge and a need for recognition inspired an Alpine-style racing series for telemarkers: the Summit Series. First it was just for fun; then it got serious. Racers were required to make telemarks and were penalized for any technical transgressions. Those interested in honing their Alpine technique stayed out of the gates — or off the piste.

Free-heel skiing continues to grow. To mountaineers and backcountry skiers telemarking satisfies the special appeal of doing more with less. It is a departure from the norm. It is a challenge. And most important, it is fun.

The Battle of the Bindings has come full circle. Alpine and Nordic skiers now carve turns on the same terrain. Accomplished free-heel skiers are mastering Alpine techniques. Less popular are the labels, the "schools." As Nansen wrote, ". . . nothing steels the willpower and freshens the mind as skiing. This is something that develops not only the body but also the soul — it has far deeper meaning for a people than many are aware of. . . ."

DENALI

It was a cold, drizzly morning on Denali's Muldrow Glacier. Although we had almost twenty-four hours of daylight, we were in a hurry to be off before the snow got too soft. Soon we would have to go on the night shift, moving in the evening when the sun's low arc left long, cold shadows.

Gearing up that morning was epic. It was like that every day. It was too late to say it, but the problem was the array of equipment we had chosen. Most of the group had prototype Ramer randonnée bindings — the very first — and there lay the problem: the bindings still had a few bugs. When they worked perfectly they were better than our Nordic setup because the stiffer boots and wider skis gave more control. But they never worked perfectly.

Two of us were using old double-Galibier touring boots, the only ones available in 1975. We had edged Nordic skis and heavy steel cable bindings. Our equipment was simple — all we had to do was step in, bend over, and flip the front throw. We had none of the others' pre-releases, iced binding mechanisms, or hinges to grease. But our system was far from perfect.

High on the mountain, we left our skis behind. It was a good thing we judged the boilerplate unskiable. The mountain was winning as, one by one, our

Bela Vadasz in the Dana Couloir
Photo by Larry Proser

9

mountaineering bindings fell apart. Our ugly-duckling Nordic gear — nothing fancy, just simple and dependable — held fast. Still, I was relieved with the failures; I didn't want to ski those hard, exposed slopes.

I had expected that since my boots could flex, my feet would be warmer. I had no idea how cold that mountain really was; over 16,000 feet my boots were frozen solid. I clumped along just like everybody else. We reached the summit in good weather, but it was still brutally cold. My feet were on the edge. I wiggled my toes unconsciously; I couldn't stop if I had wanted to. It was the one time I would have gone for a pair of those huge, goofy "mouse" boots. Summit time was brief; a few photos and we started squeaking down, crampons noisy in the cold névé.

The glacier descent was long — eighteen miles — and uneventful. We were so terrified of crevasses we used our skins when descending the lower slopes. Cracks were everywhere, creaking and groaning. Now it was too warm.

Our skis were like snowshoes. I began wondering why we had taken skis at all — because we just didn't know when to quit? Used just for transportation, they were unwieldy and undependable. But I wanted to make them work for mountaineering, to find the gear and adventures that were the ideal match. There was great room for improvement.

FREE-HEEL EQUIPMENT

My first backcountry Nordic skis were wide wooden ones, with pressed-wood edges running their full length and screwed-on metal Marius edges underfoot. The bindings were cable "beartraps" usable with touring boots or heavy leather mountaineering boots. I wore the mountaineering boots mostly for warmth. It was a noisy outfit: click, shhhh, click, shhhh, and a real blister-machine. The boots weren't great for turning, either, unless the snow was soft. But they got me into the remote winter wilderness, and they inspired me to telemark.

Today boots and skis are lighter, "faster," and more technically sophisticated. Equipment has become specialized. Many enthusiastic shoppers make a hobby of buying every possible variety of gear. Don't worry, you won't need several sets of gear to be a good free-heel skier. One Nordic outfit, properly assembled, will serve you well in a surprisingly wide variety of situations.

You want to get out and ski, but first you should learn a little about skis,

which will help you simplify your equipment selection. Otherwise, you'll spend days buying your gear and risk wasting money on the wrong stuff. Read the next section thoroughly, pick up a little of the jargon, and decide what kind of skiing you expect to do most. I'll describe the different characteristics of skis and the three major categories for backcountry and free-heel skiing. You might change your mind in the future, experimenting with another Nordic "specialty," but you can always add to your quiver at a later date.

SOME SKI TERMS

When you choose a pair of skis, you will need to know about the skis' side-cut, camber, and flex.

SIDE-CUT
Skis for turning need side-cut. In 1861 Sondre Norheim began cutting a concave arch into the sides of his wooden skis. This arch formed a narrower midsection for the skis, called the "waist,"

Sidecut ski

Camber

giving them wider tips and tails. By applying body weight to the edge of a side-cut ski, the waist presses down to contact the snow, forming a bend—an arc—in the ski.

CAMBER

Camber is the concave arch in the center of the ski. There are two general types of camber, Alpine and Nordic. Nordic camber has a more arched and stiffer section in the center of the ski, which forms a wax "pocket." Kick wax that grips the snow is applied to this area of the ski. The center wax pocket is pushed down onto the snow for purchase. This is the skier's "kick." When gliding, the skier's weight is distributed on the faster, glide-waxed tips and tails.

Alpine and cross-country downhill skis have an "Alpine" camber that distributes weight evenly over the entire running surface. With the correct Alpine camber you get a "rebound" effect from turn to turn. When flexed, Alpine-cambered skis should form a

smooth arc, with no bumps, wiggles, or wax pockets. When squeezed together base-to-base most Alpine-cambered skis are easy to close and have no resistant wax pocket.

FLEX

Ski flex most commonly refers to the longitudinal flexibility of a ski. It's discussed a lot among skiers. Usually it's bull, like forecasting the next snowfall. For turning, a softer-flexing ski arcs more easily, especially in soft snow, but it is usually less stable in harder conditions. Stiffer skis are more stable and will edge better on hard snow, but they are usually slow-turning and tiring to ski in powder. I prefer "medium" ski flex for good performance in a variety of conditions.

TORSION

Another type of ski flex is torsional—how resistant is a ski to twisting around its long axis? Torsionally rigid ski construction is needed to hold an edge on hard snow and scribe a clean arc through difficult crud. Metal layers, wood cores, fiberglass wraps, and torsion boxes are all components that contribute to torsional rigidity.

TYPES OF SKIS

There are three general types of backcountry Nordic skis: lightweight, edgeless touring skis for travel over better trails and longer distances; edged touring skis with Nordic camber for more rugged tours and heavier loads; and edged telemark skis for free-heel downhill skiing (either hiking up to ski down or lift skiing).

TOURING SKIS

This is the lightest kind of backcountry equipment: edgeless touring skis with arched Nordic camber. Of course you can tour on skis with metal edges, but edgeless skis are faster across the flats because there are no metal edges to collect ice. A pair of edgeless skis' Nordic camber is well suited to kicking and gliding. A good pair weighs from four to five pounds.

When choosing a backcountry touring ski, be sure that it has just the right amount of Nordic camber. If a ski has too much camber it always feels slippery. You may even find yourself waxing one color softer than everyone else. If it has too little camber it will be slow and won't hold wax. To test touring skis for camber, hold the skis base-to-base and squeeze them together—you should feel the resistance of the Nordic camber but be able to close them at the base with both hands.

A better method for testing camber is to put the skis on a very flat surface and stand on them where the bindings will be placed. Slide a piece of paper under one foot. With your weight evenly distributed on both skis you should be able to pull the paper out from under your foot easily. Switch all of your weight onto one foot, and the paper should be held firmly by the ski. This test will show whether you have enough body weight to contact the snow with your kick wax.

Touring skis should have side-cut. A lightweight edgeless ski should have at least eight to ten millimeters of it. If you plan to ski off-trail your skis should be at least fifty millimeters wide at their waist. If they are any narrower they will be too skimpy for support in unconsolidated (soft) snow.

Touring skis with good torsional rigidity will provide downhill stability even without edges. Check the skis' construction: metal layers, wood cores, and fiberglass-wrapped cores are all features that contribute to torsional rigidity. The skis' overall flex should be "medium" (ask a salesperson if you can't judge this for yourself) with a softer, forgiving tip.

Rick Ridgeway, John Wasson, and the author
comparing equipment notes in the Sierras
Photo by Michael Kennedy

What about waxless skis? Yes, they are much easier to use. But in cold, dry, easy-waxing climates waxless skis sacrifice glide and turnability for the lack of hassle with wax and skins. In the Rockies, waxing is easy enough to justify using waxable skis. Non-wax models are best suited for areas with warmer conditions, wet snow, and temperatures that are close to thirty-two degrees Fahrenheit.

If you do decide to go waxless choose a negative patterned base, one that is cut *into* the ski. Stay away from positive waxless patterns that protrude beyond your ski-base level—they are literally a drag.

There is a great deal of research being done on new base materials that work with the snow, like wax, through crystalline bonding. It's worth giving these new materials a try, especially if they are proven in your region's snow climate. Just be sure that your base works in conditions close to freezing—that's usually why tourers choose a waxless base.

HEAVY-LOAD, RUGGED-TERRAIN TOURING SKIS

One of the beauties of free-heel skiing is that you can head into the backcountry looking for the downhills, climbing up through meadows and over

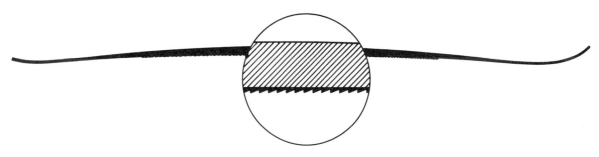

A non-wax base

peaks and passes to ski in virgin snow. Usually you carry a bigger load, whether you are laden with mostly "edible" weight for a spring picnic at the bottom of your favorite bowl or whether you're carrying equipment for a night out.

Like your load, the skis that are best-suited for venturing farther off the track are heavier. The right choice is edged skis with Nordic camber. This type of ski will also work fine for the occasional day of lift skiing at a resort, but they are really designed for long, rugged tours that require both kick-and-glide and downhill performance. They should have eight to twelve millimeters of side-cut, and be about fifty-five millimeters wide at the waist. They should be torsionally rigid for turning stability in all types of snow conditions. Depending on their construction, these skis will weigh from five to six pounds. Waxless models are available from some manufacturers in this type of ski — just be sure to read the waxless comments in the touring-ski section to find out if you are a candidate.

TELEMARK SKIS

Since a Nordic-cambered ski has a stiffer midsection that forms the wax pocket, the stiffness interferes with the smooth "line" of the ski when it's flexed into an arc for a turn. So if you ski mostly downhill either using lifts or climbing up, you will want Alpine-cambered "telemark" skis. When pressured and steered into a turn, Alpine-cambered skis flex in one smooth arc with no flat spot.

The compromise for this downhill performance? On the trail, Alpine-cambered skis are slower gliding when waxed. But there are a few lighter-weight models that are nonetheless suitable for backcountry skiing.

Alpine-cambered skis come in various flexes, or degrees of stiffness. Softer ones are for soft snow, stiffer ones for hard snow. If you prefer to ski "out of bounds" or off-piste in untracked snow then choose a softer tele ski. A "medium" overall flex provides stability in a variety of snow conditions. On-piste lift skiers and tele racers should choose skis with a stiffer flex, especially in the tail. This will contribute to the skis' stability on packed downhill runs and provide a snappy "rebound" from turn to turn.

Alpine-cambered tele skis range in weight from 5.5 to 7 pounds. Tip widths of the better skis are at least sixty-eight millimeters, some as wide as eighty millimeters. In my opinion, the wider the better, as long as they have plenty of side-cut—twelve to twenty millimeters' worth.

Many free-heel skiers use downhill skis with cables or three-pins. In soft snow they work well, but if snow conditions are hard, they will be a pretty "skiddy" setup. You don't have enough leverage with most tele boots to hold an Alpine ski on its edge. If you ski a lot of hard snow, stick to a telemark ski that's around sixty millimeters underfoot.

Have a knowledgeable salesperson show you a few skis and how to flex them. Getting them on snow is the real acid test, but in the shop you can get an idea of the range of ski flexes that are available.

Some other points to check with metal-edged skis:

Metal edges should be offset with the edges protruding beyond the sidewall so they can be side-filed for sharpening and deburring.

The groove in the base of the ski stabilizes it when it is running flat. At low touring speeds the groove makes it easier to glide on one flat-running ski. When downhill racers glide on a flat ski to gain maximum speed the groove lends stability. But grooves aren't necessary for turning. In fact, some skiers believe grooves inhibit a ski's turning ease in soft snow. Nordic-cambered skis are for kick-and-glide skiing as well as turning, so they should have a groove. With Alpine-cambered tele skis, which are meant to be skied on edge most of the time, a groove isn't necessary. You'll also find that skis without a groove are much quicker to scrape after hot-waxing.

Skis need a solid mounting plate or wood laminate underfoot to properly hold the threads of binding screws. I recommend "tapping"—pre-threading—all screw holes with a number twelve ski-service tap. This is a mandatory procedure for mounting skis with a metal topsheet, and regardless of ski construction it can reduce delamination under the binding. Any properly equipped Alpine or Nordic ski shop should be set up to do this.

If possible, you should try before you buy. Often ski shops and manufacturers offer demo programs for potential customers. It's better to pay a little more for this service than to commit your hard-earned money to a pair of mystery skis.

SKI LENGTH

The old-time "classic" touring ski length is measured with a ski in hand; a proper-length ski will reach from the floor to your wrist when your arm is fully upraised. Unless you plan to tour only in deep snow, I recommend backcountry skis at least five centimeters shorter than this norm. You can calculate this length by adding twenty-five centimeters to your height.

For telemarking, use this formula (height plus twenty-five centimeters)

for recreational telemark and backcountry skiing. If you only ski the steep and deep—especially in tight places—I recommend choosing a wide telemark ski in a length closest to your height plus twenty centimeters.

BOOTS

If you have more than one pair of anything it should be boots. Footwear is the most specialized ski gear of all. You can tour on a pair of tele skis by simply working a little harder, waxing a little thicker, or stopping and putting on skins. But touring in a pair of stiff, high-performance downhill Nordic boots can be misery. Although plastics are being used more and more in telemarking boots, leather models are still best in the backcountry. Leather is the only material that can comfortably flex forward stride after stride, breathe, and stay supple in extreme cold.

The three-pin holes of a Nordic boot are the Achilles' heel of the system. The marriage of those little holes and the binding's three pins is what takes

Lightweight backcountry boots

Heavier duty
backcountry telemark boots

all the stress of kicks, glides, turns, and head plants. Be sure that your boots either have a secure, molded-in metal plate that reinforces the pinholes or an exterior reinforcing plate installed properly by a boot-repair shop. Check the pinholes for erosion after each tour. It's really frustrating to set off and, miles away from the car, start kicking your ski off with every other stride or turn.

Backcountry boots should be comfortable for hiking or "skinning" up to your favorite descent as well as perform well on the downhills. The fit should feel like that of a good hiking boot, with plenty of toe room. Many skiers just use their old, broken-down tele boots. All boots should have "sewn" uppers, whether they are modern, inside-fastened boots with form-fitting *cemented* outsoles or outside-fastened soles using the traditional Norwegian welt. You may have to ask to see a cross-section of the boot; some cemented soles look as though they are mold-

ed. Stay away from boots with cheap injection-molded soles, which tend to fall off.

Boots for resort telemarking should be as laterally stiff as possible for edge control, with good fore-to-aft flexibility in the sole for telemark turning. For both resort skiing and backcountry skiing, boots with polyurethane midsoles don't "noodle" like those with only leather or rubber midsoles. The uppers of these telemarking boots should be higher than the touring model, with added stiffening. It's in these models that plastics are used abundantly—and appropriately. Unlike leather, plastic doesn't soften with use.

The telemarking boot's stiffer cuff should fit closely to your leg so the height and stiffness can respond to your movements. The forefoot should be snug enough to hold your foot securely. Remember, however, that you should be able to make teles by the dozens without smashing your toes. Be sure that you have enough toe room to flex

High-performance
resort-telemarking boots

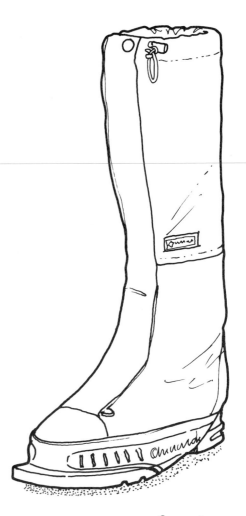

Supergaiters

forward into the tele position with little or no lift in the heel.

BOOT CARE

To waterproof your boots, use a wax-
based waterproofer that does not soften
heel counters and toe boxes. Avoid
silicone, as it may undermine the glue
bond between your boots' soles and uppers. I also use a welt sealing prepara-
tion. Up-and-down movements of
leather Nordic boots tend to "pump"
water through the welt stitching and
into your socks. To preserve their
shape and comfort, store your boots
with boot trees.

Gaiters should form a secure seal
around your boots' uppers. Choose a
pair that cover as much of the boot
laces as possible, a vulnerable area. I
like "supergaiters" that cover the entire
boot right down to the welt. The best
supergaiters are those that are held securely in place by a rubber rand. In
cold weather they add a great deal of
insulation and in soggy spring snow
they are the only way to keep your feet

dry from the outside. If you use the
rubber-rand kind, when they are not in
use either preserve the boots' shape
with boot trees or pop your rands off of
your boot toes so the rubber's tension
doesn't curl your boots

BINDINGS

Three-pin bindings offer a simple, no-
nonsense attachment of boot to ski.
There are many degrees of quality
available in three-pin bindings. Choose
a strong, dependable model made from
a heat-treated aluminum alloy. It

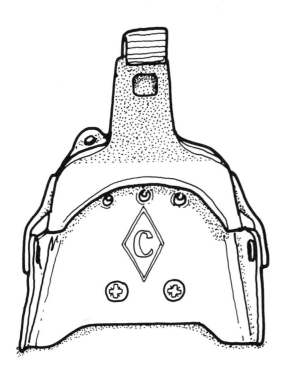

A heavy-duty three-pin binding

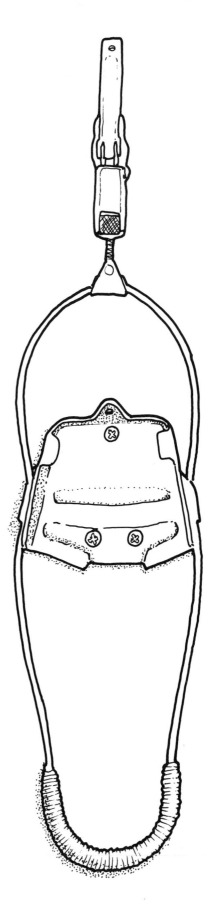

A modern cable binding

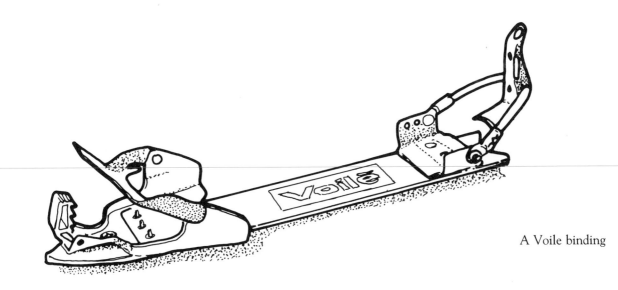

A Voile binding

should have a sturdy, riveted bail that holds your boots well back on the welt for secure boot retention and optimum ski control. It should also be adjustable for different boot-sole thicknesses.

A broken bail or ripped-out pinholes can be difficult or nearly impossible to repair with wire and duct tape. To avoid this dilemma many skiers use cable bindings for remote tours. They eliminate the dependence on three pins, plates, and pinholes for tours far off the beaten track. And the cable adds more torsional rigidity to the boot for downhill control. The price you pay? More parts means more things can go wrong. Before leaving on your trip check to see that your cables are the right size for your boots and be sure that the cables are securely strapped together with the skis for transport. On long tours carry a spare cable in your repair kit.

The Voile binding, a plastic plate that fastens under the binding and clips onto your boot heel, serves the same purpose as the cable binding. The Voile will preserve your boot toes and add torsional control to your boot/ski system. Voile also makes a retrofit release mechanism for three-pin bindings. It is designed to reduce injuries from tips hooked on the gates during races. The release system definitely adds more paraphernalia to your Nordic downhill system, but if safety is a priority over simplicity the Voile Releasable is an excellent choice. I'm sure we will see more releasable bindings for telemarking in the future.

POLES

Alpine and telemarking poles are used mainly for timing and balance. The chief purpose of Nordic poles is propulsion. Backcountry poles must do it all. To be effective, poles must be of different lengths for uphill and downhill. Poles for propulsion are of the longer, classic touring length. On the downhills you want a shorter, Alpine-length pole to allow you to use the proper hand position so you don't wave your arms high in the air.

You can have your choice with adjustable poles, which can be lengthened on the uphills and flats, shortened on the downhills, and used in two different lengths for traverses. The best adjustment system is a cam-lock arrangement that tightens and loosens by means of a cam twisted within the upper shaft.

Poles need comfortable, easy-to-hold grips that give good purchase to gloves and mittens. They should also have breakaway straps to help prevent shoulder injuries caused by a snagged basket and a sudden stop. Medium-sized baskets work best for most snow conditions; large ones have a heavy swing weight in the long haul and lift inordinate amounts of snow.

My preference for pole-shaft material in the backcountry is tempered aluminum. It's light, relatively inexpensive, and bends before it breaks. It lacks the notch-sensitivity of fiberglass. Two alloys prevail: 7075 T-6 and 7001. Both are strong, although 7075 is less expensive and is less brittle.

Few high-tech fiberglass-laminate racing-type poles are robust enough for the backcountry. If you choose a fiberglass pole for skiing in the woods buy one that is heavy duty and specially designed for serious mountain touring.

POLE LENGTH

"Classic" cross-country pole length can be calculated in centimeters by multiplying your height in inches by 2.04. This is the length that is most appropriate for touring. Alpine and telemarking pole length is easily calculated as 70 percent of your height. Another way to calculate the right length is to flip a pair of Alpine poles upside down and grab them right below the basket. With your elbows down, your arms should form a right angle

SKINS

Climbing skins are used for uphill purchase. On long uphill hauls—especially with a load—skins are the best way to save energy. They give a very positive grip, yet pull them off and you have a clean pair of skis to enjoy the downhill run.

In the old days skins were made from strips of sealskin strapped to the skis with the fur pointing backward. When striding forward the hairs would lie down and allow the ski a little glide.

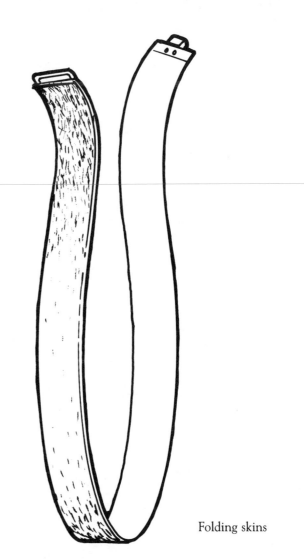

Folding skins

When pushing back, the hairs stood up and gripped the snow.

Today, most skins are made from either natural mohair or nylon. There are also several kinds of strap-on arrangements of metal, plastic, or nylon. But the best kind of skin attachment uses adhesive. The skins are treated on the back with an adhesive that can be applied, peeled off, and re-applied several times before being re-treated with adhesive.

Why is adhesive better? Snow does not collect between the skin and the ski because the adhesive is stuck to the base. The skin does not twist sideways on traverses. And the edges can be exposed for the full length of the ski on icy traverses.

You can use adhesive skins on either narrow or wide Nordic skis. The skins should be at least half of your ski's width for sufficient purchase—I prefer a width that covers the ski edge-to-edge at it's narrowest point. The skins come in lengths and should be trimmed for your skis according to the manufacturer's recommendations.

You do need to maintain adhesive skins in order to get the best performance from them. Both skis and skins should be kept clean to prevent con-

tamination of the adhesive. Because the adhesive sticks better if it is not too cold, in very cold weather skins are best warmed in the sun or next to the body before using them. Carry and store the skins by folding the adhesive back on itself.

We can talk about gear forever, but it's worthless if you don't use it. Just remember that you will never regret choosing the best gear you can afford. Ask for help from a knowledgeable friend or a trusted shop employee. Buy the kind of gear that suits you best. Then get out there and use it.

2
BASIC TECHNIQUES: YOUR FOUNDATION

WEDGE TURNS

"Jump up, cut, and dig 'em in"—that's the way one student of mine described how to turn Alpine skis. He wasn't far off, but with today's skis you needn't exaggerate quite that much to pull off a good turn.

One contributing factor to easy turning is your ski's shape and how much side-cut it has. Since the waist of a side-cut ski is narrower than the tip and tail, when the ski is put on its edge and weighted it will flex into an arc. Form that arc while moving and your ski will describe a turn.

But to make turns wherever you want you need more than just side-cut. If you simply put your skis on their edges without giving them any other help you will make a turn that's too big for a narrow backcountry couloir—or for most ski resorts' smooth trails, for that matter. To tighten up the turns, the skier's skills come into play: adding or reducing pressure on the skis, making them easier to turn; turning them by "steering" them actively with the feet; and using the skis' edges. This book is designed to help you develop those skills.

I've talked about the roots of the techniques you're about to learn. And if you've read the section about equipment you've selected the right gear. So let's get on to some skiing!

First, your body position. You'll need to maintain an effective athletic stance throughout all these techniques—a stable, relaxed, in-balance position that frees your body to act and react quickly and easily. Try it: relax your back muscles and "cup" your abdomen, pulling your navel in toward your backbone.

There is no substitute for a round, relaxed back for a balanced body position. Rock back and forth from your toes to your heels. Now try it the wrong way: arch your back, tense it, and rock back and forth. Which way feels more balanced? Which way would you catch a basketball? There's no substitute for a round, relaxed back.

I always use this athletic stance. I think especially hard about it whenever

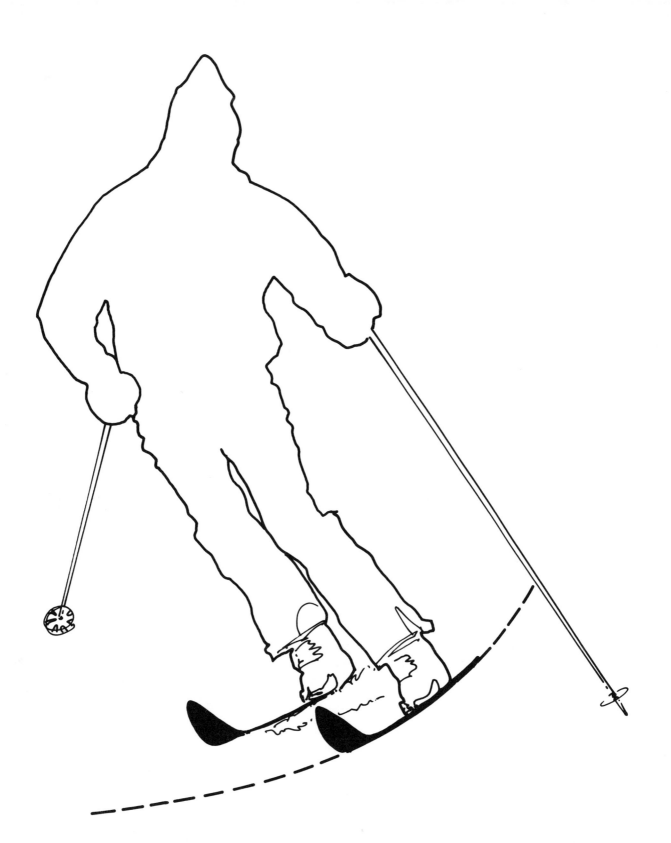

The arc inscribed by a sidecut ski

the skiing is difficult. It's a familiar focus to rely on, one that always works. When I lose my balance to the rear, this stance helps me get out of a desperate position — the "back seat." It "collects" my body into a stable, strong position.

Wedge turns are the most important turns you will learn. You'll always fall back on them, even after you've mastered telemark and parallel turns. You'll use them daily to get on lifts and to avoid other skiers or to pick your way down a corniced ridge. Ski patrollers use wedge turns to control their sleds and to get injured skiers safely down the hill. Unlike most other turns, wedge turns allow you to change direction and slow down at the same time — even through the fall line. Learn them well.

I used a term that might be new to you: *fall line*. The fall line is the direction a ball would roll when tossed down a slope. It's gravity's choice, the most direct downhill-sloping path.

Find a gentle slope with a good run-out, ski-packed or groomed for easier turning. Pick an obstacle-free fall line on your slope. Start with the correct body position, your athletic stance: stomach in, back round and relaxed, ankles flexed with knees forward. Keep your eyes on the road ahead — not at your ski tips.

Point your skis down the hill, keeping them parallel at hip width. Ready . . . Go! Push off with your poles for momentum. When you get a little speed push your heels out — just your heels — keeping your toes pointed inward and your ski tips a few inches apart. Don't worry about using your edges; just let your skis glide. Are they in a wedge? That's it, push those heels out and glide to a stop.

It's important when using a wedge not to lock your knees together. Keep them apart, as though you were riding a horse or holding a soccer ball between them. If your tips want to cross begin your wedge with your feet farther apart at hip width. To slow down, push

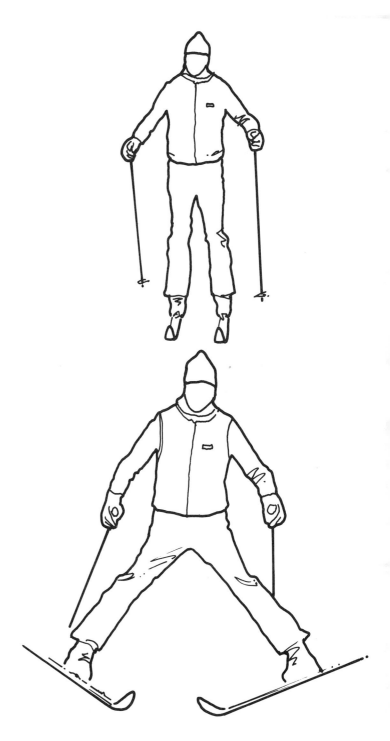

out on your heels and widen the wedge. This is the classic snowplow position—the *braking* wedge. You can see how it got its name. As your feet widen your skis tip over more onto their edges. This "edging" puts on the brakes. Use this wedge width to vary the braking action—wider for more braking, narrower for less. Just take care to avoid locked knees. If your skis seem wishy-washy and wobbly, "tighten" your feet and ankles to get the best grip from your wedged, on-edge position. Don't roll your ankles inward, just tighten them, pressing on your inside edges. Now vary the wedge. Go back forth from a narrow wedge with more glide to a wide wedge with more edge and braking action. Feel your speed change as increased edging slows you down, decreased edging speeds you up. Imagine that a tree just appeared in front of you and make an emergency stop.

Try a turn. Again, let your skis run to get some momentum, but this time use a narrow *gliding* wedge to keep your

Wedge to a stop

Wedge turn

speed — stay off the brakes. Exaggerate the wedging movement with one foot; press harder as you wedge it. Think of squashing a bug under the ball of your foot. You will turn in the direction that your squashing foot is pointing. In a wedge the toes of the right foot are pointing left, so squashing with your right foot turns you left. The left foot is pointed right, so a squash with your left foot will send you in that direction. To turn the other way, shift your weight and pressure to the other foot. Squash another bug. It works.

From now on, in all of your turns, I'll refer to this turning foot (and ski) as the *outside* foot or ski because it is on the outside of your turn's arc. You will also hear this foot called the *downhill* foot — it is on the downhill side at the turn's finish.

To link your turns, gather some speed and make shallow little arcs. Turn only with your feet, not with your

Linked wedge turns

upper body. Alternate squashing feet, shifting pressure from one foot to another. Be sure to keep your ankles and knees flexed and relaxed. Make some snaky S curves down the hill. Try controlling your speed with repeated turns. Get up some steam at the top then try to slow down by turning in a narrow, gliding wedge. Even when you use less edging, turning out of the fall line will slow you down.

Now make another run and widen your wedge, controlling your speed with your edges. See how with more edge you can make bigger turns with more time in the fall line while still controlling your speed? You've got it! You have now used the braking wedge, the gliding wedge, and the wedge turn.

BASIC TELEMARK TURNING

My first experience telemarking was in 1971, on the little town ski area north of Gunnison, Colorado. I don't remember much about it, just some confusion about which foot went forward. I do remember my skis, a narrow pair of wooden Splitkeins.

My next memory is more vivid. It was a few days later, in Crested Butte. The day was perfect, warm and sunny on Snodgrass Mountain. There were five or six inches of light snow on a firm base.

I picked a nice-looking slope, waxed my skis, and packed a good climbing track up the hill. By then I had figured out which foot to put forward, but the first couple of times I stuck out a lead ski not much happened. Just huge arcs to a stop. Then it worked. I turned my front foot a little more and made my first telemark. What a feeling! I could only turn one way, though, so my next goal was to copy my movements in the other direction.

Why had I chosen to learn telemark? Because I wanted to do everything on one kind of ski. I was a fledgling ski tourer and Alpinist. I wanted to learn techniques that I could use for touring and approaching climbs. I wanted to be stable skiing downhill on skinny skis. And I was a student. I only had time to practice one kind of skiing.

I sold my Alpine and mountaineering skis and for the next several years I only skied telemark.

Sondre Norheim first used his telemark to give himself a stable landing after a long jump. Norheim no doubt was seeking a landing stance that would allow him more fore-to-aft stability, a position that would help him resist the tremendous pull of momentum and gravity on his upper body as his skis contacted the slope.

You don't have to be a jumper to appreciate the tele. For most free-heel skiers the tele is the best choice for cruddy snow, very deep powder, or skiing any conditions that yank your feet back while throwing your body forward. The telemark's semi-kneeling, genuflecting position has superior fore-to-aft stability. It "braces" the skier to help prevent uncomfortable forward falls. Telemarks are useful in easier conditions, too. Gliding down flat terrain you can steer a tele at much slower speeds than you can a parallel turn. This low-speed telemark works wonders with a loaded pack, when a parallel turn's unweighting movements become ponderous and difficult.

Had I known an easy method for learning this enigmatic turn I might have been saved a lot of frustration. I know now that it is easiest to learn telemarks, or any ski turn for that matter, through a logical progression of skills. Try this "skill progression" — you'll learn the telemark position, the lead change, the half-wedge turn, and then the basic tele turn. If you take enough time with each skill they will all work like building blocks toward your goal.

THE TELEMARK POSITION

You'll need a good practice slope. The best practice terrain is a ski-area beginner's slope that is well packed and groomed. If you are lucky the slope will have a slow-moving lift. If a lift is not available find a gentle slope with a flat, obstacle-free runout. Pack the loose snow by side-stepping up and down the slope.

Start off with the telemark stance, using your athletic body position: a round, relaxed back and a cupped stomach. Sink into a tele. Sink straight down, sliding one foot forward and one foot back. Your weight should stay *evenly distributed* between both feet. If you see your shadow on the snow you should see "double nineties": both legs bent at near-ninety-degree angles. You will feel the weight resting on your whole front foot and on the ball of your rear foot.

The telemark position

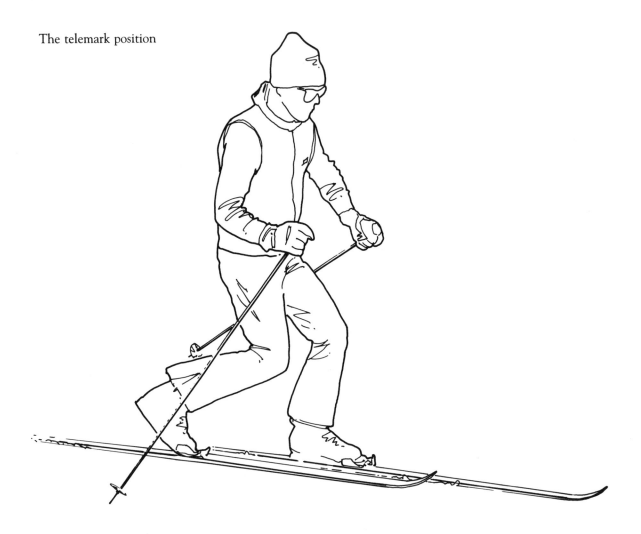

LEARNING THE TELEMARK FROM A HALF-WEDGE

The half-wedge turn is an excellent way to develop good telemark habits from the start. My first exposure to this approach was through my PSIA Nordic Demonstration Team Coach. Our coach, a long-time downhill instructor, showed us how this Alpine-style idea was likely to avoid the classic bad habits that plague the neophyte telemarker. He was right; after witnessing many telemark successes, I'm convinced.

Begin with a straight run on your practice slope. Point one ski straight and wedge the other ski out. Don't weight the wedged ski too much; you should feel its edge lightly "brush" against the snow. Your weight remains on the straight-running ski. But although your weight is on your straight-running ski, the pressure that develops on the wedged ski initiates a slight direction change. To make turns, press harder against the wedged ski. Try changing direction on either side, keeping most of the weight on the straight-running ski but pressing against that wedged one.

From now on I'll refer to the straight-running ski as your *inside* ski, since it's the ski on the inside once you

The half wedge

Half-wedge turns

make a turn. The wedged ski I'll call the *outside* ski—it's the turning ski on the outside of the arc.

Make S curves, rhythmically linking shallow half-wedge turns. In each new turn, as your weight moves to the new inside ski, the outside ski's edge brushes the snow and pulls you into a turn. You'll have the sensation that your legs are swinging back and forth under your body.

Time out for a couple of new terms. First: *steering*. Steering is physically turning your ski—I call it "pointing" the ski with your foot. If you didn't already learn it in the wedge-turn section, the second term is the *fall line*. It's the line a ball would take if you rolled it down a hill. When skiers say "step into the fall line," or "face down the fall line," we mean "step directly down the hill," or "face down the hill."

THE TELEMARK TURN

The transition from half wedges to telemarks is the next step. Begin making half-wedge turns. To make a telemark, add a move to the half-wedge initiation: as you wedge the outside ski slide it forward and sink into the telemark stance (the same stance that you practiced earlier). Steer (twist) the advanced front ski through a turn. Practice one tele turn at a time, beginning in a traverse and turning uphill to a stop. Sink *between* your feet, with both skis equally weighted. Practice this "stop-turn" in both directions.

When you become more comfortable with your stop turns in each direction you should practice a "garland." The exercise is named for the pattern your skis scribe in the snow. It's a very useful way to develop confidence in your

Half wedge to telemark

turns. Step into the fall line a little more each time you begin a stop turn. Each turn starts with a steeper traverse until finally there is no traverse at all. Once you are comfortable turning without a traverse, start facing directly down the hill, beginning the stop-turn in the fall line.

LINKING TURNS

Try linking some wedge teles down a shallow slope. Combine the two movements of wedging and sinking into one: rather than wedging the outside ski and *then* sinking into the telemark—two distinct movements—sink into the telemark position at the same time you wedge your outside ski. On a gentle slope you will feel as though you are

walking "pigeon-toed" from one tele to the next.

When practicing on gentle terrain you can abbreviate the braking action of the half wedge and sink sooner into your telemark. If the terrain is steeper you will want to stay in the half wedge longer, through the fall line, before you sink into the tele finish. This will control your speed.

MOTION

With practice you can eliminate the half-wedge step and adopt a more advanced, pure telemark. The key is movement. Use your body's entire range of motion. Stand tall at the beginning of your turn—much taller than in the "classic" telemark position you

A. tele garland

first practiced. Then sink through each tele turn as you make your arc, finishing the turn in that "classic" stance. Stand up tall for the next turn, and repeat the sinking motion through the arc.

As you sink, steer and edge your front ski. Each time you initiate a new turn stand up again, sink, and steer. Weight your uphill edges — especially your front ski. Soon you'll be gracefully linking telemark turns, one after another.

BASIC ALPINE TURNING

When I heard that "The Man Who Skied Down Everest" won an Academy Award for best documentary, I wanted to see it. I went with my friend Dee, another mountaineer with a growing enthusiasm for skiing. We were really pumped after seeing the film, so we decided to go ski mountaineering the next day in the Indian Peaks. Dee had very short skis; perfect, according to him, for performing his "Washington Waddle" ski technique. Dubious. I had my old favorites: long, skinny tele boards.

With an Alpine start we climbed a moderate peak not too far from the road head. The peak had shoulders on all sides that promised to provide beautiful open-bowl skiing. First we went to the summit, relaxing on top to let the snow soften, then started down the rocky summit ridge, carrying our skis.

Dee is a lunatic. It's a good thing he's a doctor, his own mechanic. His natural bent was further inspired by the film, watching Mr. Muira butt-check at sixty miles per hour down Everest's Lhotse Face. So when we had to traverse a little snow gully along the ridge, Dee didn't have to say anything. I knew what he was thinking. I was just hoping he wouldn't say "let's ski this."

There was no way I could fit telemarks into that narrow a space. Had I had a strong parallel turn, especially with Dee's miniature skis, I might have tried. Dee was on his own. He wrestled his skis on his feet and side-slipped into the gully, shaking with what I hoped was boundless enthusiasm. I couldn't watch; I headed down the ridge to the more open slopes below.

When I left Dee was side-slipping. Below he confessed to having side-slipped most of the way down before making a turn. He said that once in the gully, its steepness had scared him witless. But lower down it widened into the bowls, a much more inviting place to commit one's body downhill.

Sure, I was relieved that he had found it difficult, which helped rationalize my "mature" decision. No one likes to admit they have chickened out.

I was envious. I'm sure that I wouldn't have turned in that gully either. But I think that had I been confident of my parallel turns, I might have tried it.

Each season I set a goal for my skiing. The next season my goal was free-heel parallel turns. I skied as much as possible with Alpine skiers, watching and mimicking them. I began to use parallel turns in more varied conditions. First I practiced parallel only on hard snow, making the most of the technique's stable side-to-side stance. As my turns became stronger I mixed them up, using them where *least* appropriate, trying to strengthen my parallel turns in powder and crud.

It worked. By the end of the season my parallels were coming around. Soon I had more turns at my disposal, and more fun. Why parallel? When terrain is steep, icy, or the space very "tight" for turning, Alpine techniques—properly performed—work best. Under these conditions the anticipated stance of the parallel turn (or the hybrid tele-mark christy) works much better than the tele's rotated stance. And parallel turns are elegant; with all extraneous moves deleted they create a series of subtle, composed body angles that produce deceptively quick turns.

Teles and parallels aren't all there is. To be a versatile, go-anywhere skier on all kinds of equipment you'll need to master a variety of maneuvers: wedges, stem turns, and stem christies. These skills form an ideal learning progression for developing strong, advanced Alpine turns.

STEM TURNS

Wedging one ski to the side is called *stemming* the ski. After wedge turns, stem turns are the next step to developing your stem christy and parallel turns.

Wedge turns, linked with a traverse, are the foundation of the stem turn.

Stem turn

What's a *traverse*? A traverse is gliding across the hill using your uphill edges to maintain a horizontal course.

Now let's get on the hill. To practice a stem turn, begin with a traverse across the slope. Stem (wedge) your uphill ski—that's the one that will become the *outside* ski in the turn. As you feel the ski's edge grip the snow, press on it, twisting it even more in its turning direction. (Twisting your feet—that's called steering, turning

your ski with a twist of your foot.) This pressure and twisting should bring you into the fall line and around the turn, just as in your two-footed wedge initiation. Keep turning all the way around through the fall line. Once across the hill begin a traverse, letting your skis glide together parallel before your next stem.

Now stem the new outside ski, bring the turn *all the way* around, and let the skis glide parallel in a traverse. Check your stance. Your skis should be hip width. Be sure that you are turning with your skis, not with your body. To avoid the classic mistake of turning with your body—rotating it into the hill—avoid watching your ski tips. Keep looking down the hill, several turns ahead. Pick a distant focal point and keep your eyes on it.

Practice stem turns back and forth across the hill. I know, they feel more like an exercise than a usable skill. They are. Unlike "foundation" techniques such as the wedge, skills that you always use, the stem turn is an exercise to develop skills necessary for further advancement to stem christies and parallels. What skills? Independent foot movements, speed control, edging.

SIDE-SLIPPING

Side-slipping is skidding—releasing your edges and flattening your skis to slide sideways down the hill. Side-slipping isn't just for skills development, it's a technique. Sure, it's an important basic, but a good side slip is not only for beginners. It's crucial to pressure control in the most advanced skiing. On something steep and narrow I find that, snow allowing, a short side slip is just what it takes to gain momentum for that difficult first turn. Or, like Dee, you can make a long side slip and postpone that first turn.

Practice your side slip on a short, steep, packed slope. Begin by climbing up from the bottom, side-stepping to the top. Are your skis slipping out from under you? If so, then tip them into the hill a little more. Don't lean, just tip the skis, edging with your feet, ankles, and (to a lesser degree) your knees. Once you are a ways up the slope, try a downhill side slip. Face your body downhill: round, relaxed back, cupped stomach, head up. Then, with your skis horizontal (across the fall line), let up on your edges, rolling your feet and knees away from the hill. Your skis should side slip down the hill.

Develop control of your side slip by alternately flattening your skis and edg-

Sideslipping

ing them to come to a halt. Try to slide sideways only, with a minimum of forward motion. This will not only give you sideways mobility on steep slopes but will help you perform stem christies and parallels.

STEM CHRISTIES

I remember watching three of Hans Gmoser's helicopter guides descending from the summit plateau of Mount Logan, the highest peak in Canada's Yukon. They were skiing roped together. I watched carefully in hopes of gleaning some off-piste Alpine tricks that I could use for our free-heeled descent. To my surprise they were all making controlled stem christies. No parallels, even in the easier snow! Teles sufficed to get us down, but I wanted to know more about using the stem christy in these situations.

If you must control your speed for dicey skiing, the stem christy is the best turn. Advanced skiers use it because the stem produces a quick, controlled-turn initiation, a key to avoiding the sudden acceleration present in the first half of a parallel turn. Stem christies provide excellent side-to-side stability, an indispensable element for negotiating crevasses—especially with a big pack.

The word *christy* defines a parallel skid with both skis edged in the same direction. Stem christies combine the stemmed-turn initiation with a weight shift to the outside ski, resulting in a skidded christy or parallel finish. You initiate the stem christy as you do a stem turn, by stemming your outside ski. Once you stem the ski you step onto it—I call this move a "stem step." Both skis are then steered parallel into the christy turn finish.

Try it. As you stem the outside ski into a wedge position, stand up tall. Stand up as though you want to reach out with that stemming ski. Then step onto it, shifting your weight to the stemmed ski. Steer your skis into the fall line. Sink with your body as you steer through the turn, preparing to stand up for the next stem.

Practice first in a garland, turning only in one direction from a traverse. Unlike your first teles, there's no need

Linked stem christies

to step turn into the fall line. Let your stem bring you around. Stand up tall and stem-step, then sink and steer your turn around to a stop. Feel the flowing sensation that standing up and sinking produce as you swoop through the fall line.

The next step, linking stem christies, feels quite natural: once you steer your last turn across the fall line, stand tall and stem-step your new outside ski, shifting your weight onto it. With your weight shifted, you're now steering into your next turn.

Stand up, sink, stand up, sink—this is an important movement that I will emphasize time and time again throughout this book. It's an unweighting; the sinking lightens your skis. If you don't believe me, try it on your bathroom scale. Stand tall and sink abrubtly. Notice how your weight drops when you sink down. Your skis stay lighter, easier to steer, as long as you are sinking.

Here's another exercise: *lighten your inside ski* as you steer both skis through the fall line. Think "light as a feather" on the inside ski. This gets you steering and turning with your outside ski, the one that does most of the work in Alpine skiing. Your light inside ski will drift parallel to "match" the outside ski—forming that stable parallel christy in your turn finish. Some skiers actually lift their inside ski when they stem step to exaggerate this "lightness." (See the last figure in the illustration.)

Now, review the two points of focus that will make stem christies much easier: (1) Use plenty of up-and-down movement, starting tall and sinking through the turn; and (2) lighten the inside ski as your skis come through the fall line.

HOCKEY STOPS

With the hockey stop, you'll develop greater maneuverability and control for your parallel turns. The hockey stop's abrupt two-footed twisting and resultant two-footed skid is just an over-exaggerated version of the two-footed steering and christy of the basic parallel turn.

Practice hockey stops on a smooth slope. Standing tall, point your skis straight down the hill in a wide, stable stance. Push off for speed. Once you gain momentum, sink abruptly, flexing at the ankles and knees (not at the waist!) and steer your skis hard across the fall line. Continue facing down the hill as your skis come across the slope. Your parallel skis will skid you to a stop.

Practice hockey stops in the other direction to be comfortable stopping on either side. This is your emergency

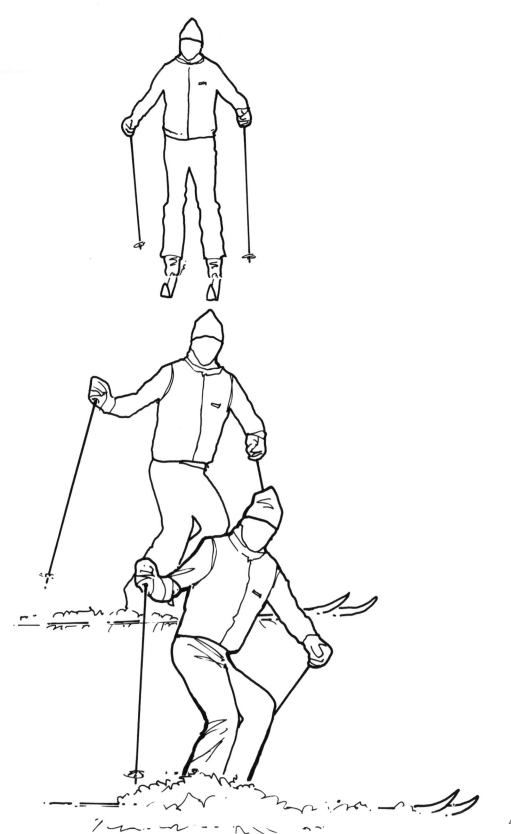

A hockey stop

stop. Just remember to practice it *below* obstacles — or your friends — to avoid dangerous collisions.

THE BASIC PARALLEL TURN

You can use parallel turns on any kind of ski equipment: Alpine, randonnée, three-pin, or cross-country racing boards. The parallel turn is to Alpine skiers what the telemark turn is to Nordic skiers: an ultimate goal. How many times I have heard an enthusiastic beginner exclaim in a southern drawl, "I want to learn to *parallel*."

Skiers learn parallel turns most easily on a smooth, well-groomed slope. Take care to use a stance no narrower than your hip width. First make some smooth stem christies standing very tall at the turn start, stem-step and sink your body deeply through the turn. (Bend at the ankles and knees, not at the waist.) Exaggerate this "vertical" motion so your skis feel light and maneuverable as you start each new turn.

Next, focus on lightening your inside ski; be sure it's light as soon as you stem-step onto your outside one. Shift your weight to the stemmed ski and bring the inside one parallel to it.

Now we're going to eliminate the stem. Pick an open area on your gentle slope with lots of room to move. Rather than stemming the outside ski first to get the turn started and *then* stepping onto it, we're going to *step first* on that ski and *then* turn it. That's right, shift your weight to your outside ski first — stepping onto it — *then* twist it, steering it into the fall line as you did in your stem christies. You are applying the twisting movements to your downhill ski *after* shifting your weight to it. This way your skis stay parallel, eliminating the wedging motion of the stem. Practice these turns one at a time as you did the stem christy, using the garland in one direction then the other.

When you step onto your outside ski be sure that you step off of the inside one, making it light and maneuverable.

A basic parallel

You can actually lift the inside ski. Just be sure to keep those parallel skis hip width—no narrower. Your skis will slide around into a parallel christy.

Don't worry if you feel a bit wobbly. With practice you will soon feel more solid. Practicing hockey stops will help solidify your two-footed steering. Remember that they are abrubt, a gross version of a parallel turn. You will want to temper those abrupt movements for these elegant parallel turns you're learning.

FLEXION AND EXTENSION

When I refer to up-and-down movement, or vertical motion, I often do so in quotes. That's because flexion and extension of your legs really doesn't create a purely up-and-down motion:

the angle of the hill makes the movement of your body fall somewhere between up and down and in and out. Either way, I can't emphasize this movement too much. In all downhill techniques "vertical" movement of the body is what makes the skis work for you. This movement allows you to control and use the pressures that gravity and centrifugal force create against your edges. It is the key to more carve and less skid.

There's a whole chapter devoted specifically to this "vertical" movement. The point is to develop a *three-dimensional* motion in your skiing—a flowing down the hill while your body moves dynamically into the fall line, extending and flexing, in and out. There are many more tips in the advanced section. Stick with it.

Extension and flexion

COURMAYEUR

I feel lucky to have a job that keeps me skiing. In fact, it has often brought me to exactly the right place at the right time. I remember so well one of those times, when I was in Italy developing some new telemark skis for Chouinard Equipment. Here's an excerpt from a letter I wrote my girlfriend that tells it best:

We're in Courmayeur, on the Italian side of Mont Blanc. We drove up from Biella yesterday afternoon. Last night I met Eberhard's friend Renzino, a long-time local guide. He offered to take us on one of the famous off-piste runs in the area. We jumped at the chance; soon enough we would be doing the jerk, mounting, tuning and testing skis.

This morning we got an Italian Alpine start: 8:30. We had to wake up the lady in our pension to get a cup of coffee. I don't believe it; if your reward for getting up early is having these incredible mountains to yourself, it's well worth it.

Eberhard is an ex-World Cup racer and speaks German as a first language. But he's very Italian. He has a great sense of humor; he loves style, change, new things. He goes nuts watching telemark skiing. In fact, that's how we met. It was in the U.S.; Eberhard wanted to learn to telemark, and some friends put him in touch with me. First day out, he never fell down.

Perfect snow for parallel turns
Photo by Michael Kennedy

59

But today I was the only skier on the hippy sticks; Eb and Renzino were Alpine skiing.

We had to ride lifts for almost an hour. I left ten pairs of randonnée and tele skis at midpoint at Val Veny to test later in the afternoon. I wondered what the off-piste would be like, not having had snow in several days.

The last cable car was a rickety old thing. I got the impression they just fired it up every few weeks for Renzino. It took us to the top, to Cresta d'Arp, they called it. We fiddled around for a few minutes; Eberhard was having trouble with his randonnée bindings. I rubbed it in at how simple mine were.

My Alpine buddies took off making some very square turns; I knew I was in for it. Breakable crust. Luckily I had grabbed a pair of skis that were a bit short, well-suited to hop and hope.

The crust didn't last for long. Still high, we cut a wide traverse toward a distant ridge. I kept glancing uphill, checking my beacon. Even though I was skiing with locals, all Europeans seem a bit brazen about traversing avalanche slopes. But soon we safely reached the ridge.

Renzino skied down first and set up his camera. It looked good, but I had no idea how good. We side-stepped over the ridge and pushed off one at a time.

The next two hundred turns were ultimate — dry, light, knee-deep. Each skier had a fresh line, cutting tight, round tracks down the steep slope. It was absolutely perfect. I had tears in my eyes at the bottom.

Our run was just starting — we descended another five thousand feet, all the way to Dolonne on the valley floor. We skied the works — powder, crud, and crust, around cliffs and through gullies. There were no sandbags, no one out to prove anything. We didn't even talk.

FREE-HEEL SKI CARE

Waxing can be as simple or as complex as you choose to make it. For back-country use, keep it simple. You may have a suitcase of wax at home, but what you take to the wilderness should fit into the palm of your hand. Not only will you save weight but decisions about the wax will be much simpler. My wilderness wax kit includes a two-wax system for kick in fine-grained snow, a universal klister for kick in re-frozen snow, and a universal glider. Combine this ultralight wax kit with a pair of stick-on skins for long, steeper climbs, and you can go just about any-where.

SIMPLIFIED WAXING

The two-wax system is easy to use. Most manufacturers offer a two-wax op-tion. Swix, for example, uses Silver for wet snow and Gold for dry. At the trail head, make a snowball. If the snow is wet enough to pack into a good, moist ball—a real window-breaker—use Sil-ver. If the snow is too dry to pack, use the harder Gold wax. "Crayon" it on the ski in the kick zone under the

binding. Start with a layer a couple of feet long, from your heel forward.

The color-coded waxing system is certainly more involved than the two-wax system. Still, it's not hard to un-derstand because the waxes are orga-nized into specific colors for specific temperatures. Greens are the coldest, Blue is in the middle, and Violet, Red, and Yellow are the warmest. I know, I said "Greens." That's because for most of the basic colors there is an Extra and a Special version of that color. Most wax manufacturers designate the Extra as one half-step warmer than its base color, the Special as one half-step cold-er. Why? The original base colors were very wide in their temperature ranges and were formulated for wood skis. The half-steps were developed to fill in these gaps as the modern synthetic ski bases—which require more specific wax—came into vogue. The half-steps are excellent, especially the Extras.

Instead of the two-wax system, I sometimes carry several Extras: Extra Green, Extra Blue, and Extra Purple. If it's warmer, I'll drop the Extra Green and carry Extra Red on the warmer end of the spectrum. These Extra waxes have a much broader temperature range than the numbers on their cans imply, and you may find them a bit more durable than the two-wax system. You can cover a broad temperature range with only two or three waxes. Apply the "three-wax Extra" system the same way as the two-wax system, using air temperature as your criterion for color selection instead of the snowball technique.

Once your skis are waxed start up the trail and test your wax job. If it works, don't fix it. If a ski slips, lengthen the "kicker" toward the tip and tail. If it still slips, add more layers, smoothing each one with a cork. Several smooth, thin layers are more effective than one thick one. And if it still slips, switch to the softer Silver wax (or a warmer Extra), starting with a smooth, thin layer again.

The penetration ability of snow (its crystals' sharpness) into hard wax is a function of temperature and water content. Wetter and warmer snow requires a softer wax which the rounded, moisture-laden snow grains can penetrate. Klister is used as a kick wax for old, refrozen snow, snow so abrasive that it necessitates a more durable, sticky wax. Klister is just as durable on your clothes as on your skis, so be careful with both the tube and the waxed skis. A zip-lock bag for unused klister is mandatory.

Klister must be applied warm—otherwise it's too difficult to get out of the tube's little orifice. If it's cold, you'll more than likely squeeze the tube too hard and get klister oozing unexpectedly from the back side of the tube. Warm the tube carefully over a torch, or carry it (in a plastic bag) inside your jacket.

Once the warmed klister is viscous, a short, sparing bead should be applied to the wax pocket of the ski. It can then be smoothed with a klister spatula or, better yet, a putty knife. Use it sparingly; less is best. If it's difficult to smooth, carefully apply a little heat to the wax with a torch or stove. I sometimes use the heel of my hand to smooth klister.

Don't worry about getting it on your hands—just put your gloves back on and deal with it later.

"Now try taking klister off," you say. I've awakened to new snow on many spring skiing trips after having applied copious amounts of klister the previous day. Armed with only a putty knife I could remove almost all traces of the sticky wax. The trick is the temperature. I cool the skis in the shade, then run the putty knife lengthwise along each ski, sliding the blade under the klister next to the base and peeling it off. The clean ski is then ready for cold wax and fresh snow.

Rounding out my backcountry system is a universal glider. Glide wax nourishes and protects a polyethylene base, preventing it from hardening and oxidizing. It protects skis when travelling. I leave a heavy coat on my skis for the trip and scrape it down once I arrive at my destination. And glide wax makes skiing easier. Not only are the skis faster up the trail but they turn more readily. Almost all turns are part-ly skidded, and glide wax makes the skid much easier.

For touring, gliders should be applied only to the tip and tail of a ski. If applied under the foot they can inhibit the adhesion of the kick wax. If skis are used for downhill only, or just with skins, the entire base should be waxed. At home that's best done with a dry iron set on medium heat. Hold the wax against the iron and drip it onto the ski. (If the wax smokes, the iron is too hot.) Then iron the wax into the ski being sure to keep the iron moving to prevent damage to the base of the ski. After the wax has cooled scrape it with a plastic scraper. In cold temperatures the wax should be almost invisible. For warm conditions the wax can be a little thicker, but it should still be scraped thoroughly.

In the backcountry you can rub glider on a ski like a kick wax and then cork it smooth. This method is not as durable as ironing but is quite effective when an outlet isn't available. I also use universal Alpine glider paste in a tube. It can be rubbed on and polished with a handkerchief.

If you want to experiment with different colors of kick wax, stick with one brand until its use is second nature. Then, if you continue to experiment, try the most popular colors in other brands. Choose a wax color by matching the temperature with the wax's temperature range printed on the can. Use the same crayoning and testing routine as with the two-wax system. Remember, backcountry waxing doesn't require an alchemist. This four- or five-wax approach satisfies the backcountry skier's need for ultralight weight with plenty of versatility.

A note about newer techniques: in firm spring conditions I have gone on long tours with no kick wax at all—just a pair of skating skis, a fanny pack, and long skating poles. This equipment was developed specifically for the (relatively) new cross-country skating technique pioneered on the World Cup circuit by Bill Koch. After Koch won the World Cup with his new technique it became quite a subject of controversy. Is it skiing? Is it unfair? How does it affect those who cannot skate? Skating technique on well-prepared tracks is so much faster than traditional technique that it was finally deemed a different "stroke." Races are now termed "classical" for traditional skiing and "freestyle" for skating.

Skating isn't just for racing. It's very effective in the backcountry, especially for long, gradual grades, those deemed interminable when striding or double-poling. But to skate you do need firm conditions. Frozen corn in the backcountry is ideal; skating in a foot of fresh powder isn't. It's plodding. So add skating technique to your repertoire, but carry kick wax—and skins—for the wide variety of conditions prevalent in the bush.

TUNING

Most of us are familiar with tuning our skiing technique, but many of us neglect our equipment. Sure, technique problems are usually caused by operator error, not the skis. But neglecting your skis' tuning can compound those errors. It doesn't take much to keep your skis properly tuned. With a few tools and a little time you can get your new skis ready to turn, or buff out your old skis as good as new. Once tuned, your skis will be much easier to maintain for optimum performance.

GETTING A FLAT BASE

Your ski's base should be flat; if part of the base is high or low you won't get the most out of your investment. Many telemark skis come excessively base-high from the factory, giving the ski bottom a convex shape. Base-high skis are squirrelly and unstable. But skis with high bases are easier to ski than those with low or concave bases; this so-called "railed" phenomenon makes any ski desperately unpredictable.

To determine if your bases are flat, first check them with a true bar—a metal bar machined perfectly flat for eyeballing bases and edges. Hold the ski up to the light and move the true bar down the full length of the ski, looking for daylight between the ski base and the bar. I prefer a black-colored true bar as it's more glare-free for my sun-weakened eyeballs. Light will show where the P-Tex base or the metal edges are "low." No light will show through spots that are flat or too high. High bases should be scraped or ground down; skis with high edges should be filed flat.

If your skis' plastic bases are excessively high it's best to have them stone-ground by a qualified tuning shop. Of course, such luxuries aren't always available. If that's the case, you can scrape the skis with a metal scraper until they are flat. To flatten a high base, hold your ski securely in ski vises and scrape the high spots down with the sharp side of a metal scraper. Tip the scraper away from you and push it using long, even strokes from tip to tail. (You can sharpen a dull scraper with a file, taking care to keep the scraper edge flat.) Be careful not to flex the

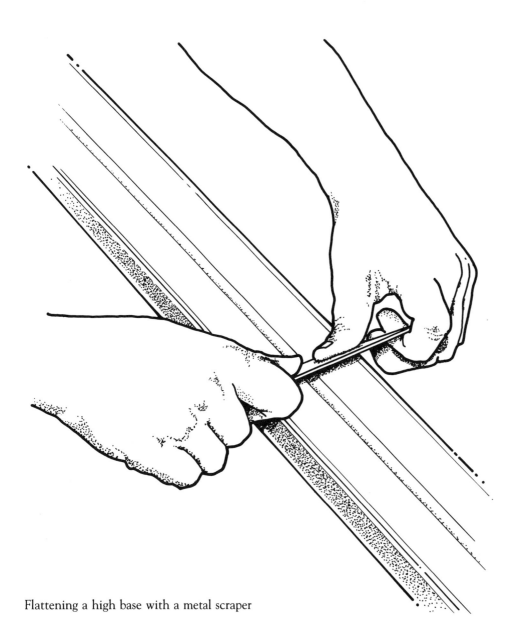

Flattening a high base with a metal scraper

scraper. You should be able to feel it grip those areas of the ski base that are too high. Check the ski base periodically to be sure you aren't removing too much P-Tex base material. Scrape until the material is perfectly flat and flush with the ski edge.

FLAT FILING

Your ski is "railed" when its edges are higher than its base. On a railed ski, light will show between the base and the true bar, but none will show between the edges and the bar. Railed skis can be desperately difficult to turn. And they will "hook" badly when skiing across the fall line. Flat filing solves the problem.

For heavy flat filing use at least a ten-inch-mill bastard file. Some prefer an auto body file or a Panser, but with these aggressive tools you must know

Checking for a flat base with a true bar

when to stop. Whichever file you choose, grip it close to the ski, placing your thumbs over the ski's edges. Be careful not to bend the file when you grip it; keep it flat. Place it on the ski at an angle so its teeth cut. You will soon get the feel of the best angle according to the design of your file. You can push or pull the file, whichever seems most comfortable, but the file's tang should always point *away* from the cutting direction.

File with long, smooth strokes. Clean the file often with the brush-side of a file card—the metal side dulls files and is best saved for hard-to-remove wax residue and plastic filings. Keep the base of the ski free of filings with a rag or brush. File the edges until they are flush with the base, checking the ski frequently with a true bar.

BEVELING THE EDGE
Alpine skiers are familiar with edge beveling: tuning the ski with its edges filed slightly lower than the level of the plastic base. Beveling is important for telemark skiers, too, since it lowers the grabby edge, making the ski easier to swivel and easing your turn initiation. Beveling reduces that "catchy" feeling so aggravating in three-pin skis and so conducive to outside edge falls. It minimizes that "too sharp" sensation in soft and crusty snow and on steep slopes. And with beveled edges you can ski

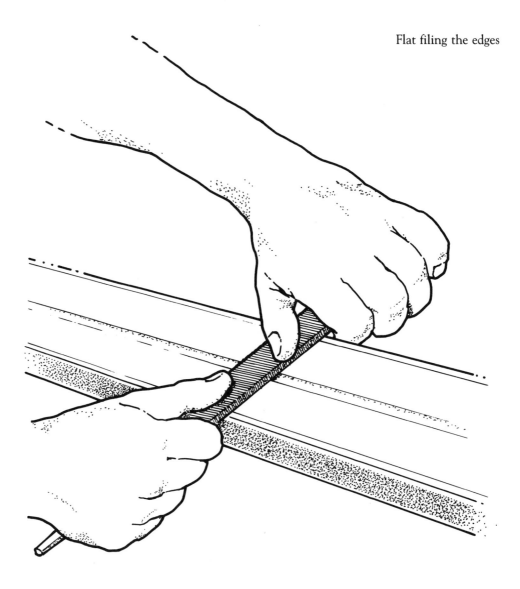

those skinny boards farther away from your body, like the big boys, rather than using an upright "Nordic" stance.

If you're willing to spend the money and have a trustworthy tuning shop nearby, you can take your skis to be stone-ground and edge-beveled precisely to your instructions. My preference is a one-degree bevel. This isn't a lot. Some Alpine skiers use up to a three-degree bevel. And many of these "combat" skiers bevel the tips and tails more

than the center of the skis. You can experiment with different degrees of bevel, but if you bevel telemark skis too much they'll have to be tipped too far over to engage the edge. Their wide Nordic bindings will drag, putting you in a desperate situation on steep, hard snow.

There is no mystery to edge beveling. If you don't have the heavy machinery to do it you have some fairly simple options. The most foolproof tool for edge beveling at home is a quality hand beveler. If you don't care to buy yet another tool, you can do an effective job with a piece of duct tape on a ten-inch file.

If you buy a hand beveler, be sure that it can bevel the base edge; many of them only bevel the side edge. If your beveling tool is adjustable I recommend setting it at one-degree for beveling the bottom edge of telemark skis. If you choose to bevel your skis more than that you should bevel the side edge, too. This keeps the edge profile close to ninety degrees for the best edge bite. Follow the instructions included with your tool for both procedures.

To bevel with a file and duct tape, carefully wrap the end of your ten-inch or twelve-inch file with two wraps of the tape. Rub the tape flat, making sure there are no raw edges or wrinkles. Place the file on the ski with the tape over one edge, the file over the other edge. The tape will lift one side of the file so that it tunes the opposite edge with a slight bevel. File with long, smooth strokes just as you flat file. You can monitor your edge bevel by the new metal that is exposed as you file. Or, if you're not sure of yourself, use a side-filing trick: color the edge with a Magic Marker before filing. Be careful to keep the ink off of your clear plastic base because it can stain it. File until the full width of the edge is beveled. It's also best to bevel into the base for about an edge-width. Now turn the file around and repeat the process on the other edge.

By taping your file carefully and replacing the tape if it packs too flat, you can do an excellent job using this method. You'll quickly get the feel of your files and how much they are cutting. Take your time and use your true bar. If you remove too much metal you'll have to scrape the base down and start all over.

SIDE FILING
The best telemark skis have offset edges like Alpine skis. When you hit a rock,

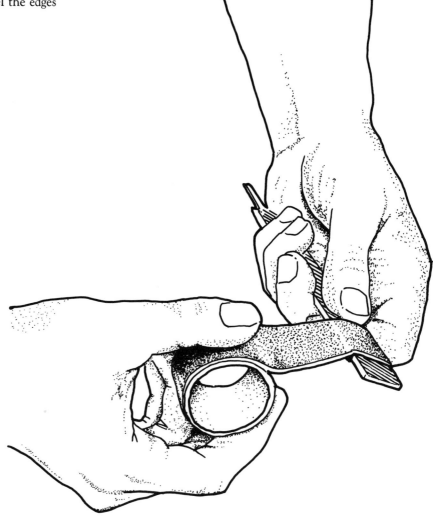

the metal edge is work-hardened by the impact. The result is a rough spot called a burr, and it's usually much harder than the rest of the edge. You may have the same problem with a new ski whose edges have been work-hardened by the manufacturer's final base grinding. With work-hardened edges you can file until you're blue in the face but you'll make little progress.

You can side-file skis with an offset edge to restore them to ninety degrees and to remove nicks or burrs. First put one of your skis firmly in a vise. You'll need both a stone and a file. Go over these areas with a stone first. You'll reduce the hard spot so that your file will bite. It's worth taking this extra step to minimize wear on yourself and your files.

If the ski has an offset sidewall as well as an offset edge, hold the file in the palm of your hand and run it lengthwise along the side edge in long,

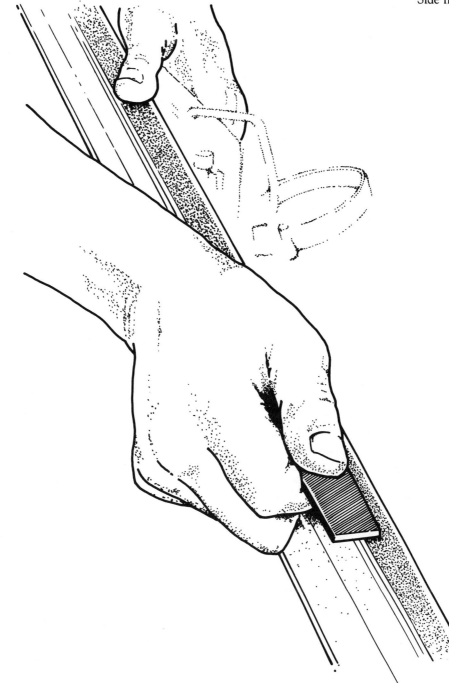

Side filing the edges

smooth strokes. Be sure to keep the file flat against the edge and sidewall. If the sidewall is not offset (not all tele-mark skis have offset sidewalls), hold the file in both hands at an angle to the edge as though you are flat filing. In this case, you will need to keep your thumbs pressed right over the edge to keep from bending the file. It is impor-tant to file evenly and perpendicular to the ski base. If the new metal is ex-posed evenly along the full width of the edge, you are doing fine. This is a great place for the Magic Marker trick: color the edge and then file the ink off evenly.

After sharpening your edges you should remove the burr created by the file and then dull the edges back from the tips and tails. The too-sharp burr will hang up the skis in turns and the skis will behave as though they were railed. I prefer a burr stick for removing this wire edge. A burr stick is a "rubber stone," like an eraser with just the right amount of abrasiveness to remove the burr without losing the keen edge.

If you have a burr stick, run it along the edges tip-to-tail. Or lightly run a fine whetstone or emery paper the full length of the edge at a forty-five degree angle to the ski base. Then use your burr stick or stone to dull the edges back fifteen centimeters from the con-tact surface of each ski's tip and tail. If you are skiing at a ski area it is a good idea to carry some emery paper or a small pocket stone. Depending on the snow, you might want to "de-tune" your ski's edges a bit more if they seem catchy.

Once your skis have been properly tuned you will never want to go back to an untuned ski. To keep them at their best, occasionally touch them up with your stone or a light side filing. Keep them sharp, especially underfoot. And stay out of the rocks.

3
ADVANCED FREE-HEEL TECHNIQUES

ADVANCED TELEMARK TIPS

When I think of a series of good tele turns, I think of a horse. I liked horses before I discovered skis. When I really wanted to get my horse—his name was John—to perform, I would first get him collected. I would rein him in, signalling him to prepare for anything: a quick turn, a jump, a skid-stop. John knew the signal. He would collect his big body into a "ready" posture rather than trotting along. His big body would perk up as though he had just seen a snake and was preparing to bolt.

TUCK YOUR REAR LEG

When making teles, you can collect yourself by tucking your rear leg under you and bringing your body into its most athletic position. Don't leave your back leg flapping in the breeze like a wounded dog (a doggie leg); keep it under you where you can use it. Your body should feel collected and ready to pounce. Be sure to avoid a too-wide stance. With your knees closer together as you tuck your rear leg under you,

you will gain that feeling of control afforded by the telemark's long-single-ski effect. Try pinching your buttocks together as though you are holding a C-note between your cheeks. Your knees will come closer together, unifying your two wandering skis into one long, stable tele board. You'll feel aggressive, ready for anything.

POINT YOUR HEADLIGHTS

Start your turns thinking of your front knee as a headlight. With each turn sweep the headlight beam toward your new destination. This focus will enhance the edging and steering of your front ski.

USE YOUR BIG TOE, LITTLE TOE FOR THE PROPER EDGE

The "big-toe, little-toe" idea is simple: when you edge your skis into a turn, feel the pressure under the big-toe side (inside) of your front foot and the lit-

Tuck your rear leg under

Opposite: Point your headlights . . .
the author in Japan
Photo by Satoshi Ishizu

tle-toe side (outside, mid-foot) of your rear foot. This will edge your skis properly. The rear ski—the little-toe ski—is especially important. Avoid "tiptoeing" on it. Keep your entire forefoot on the ski. Should you feel the rear ski sliding out from under you, concentrate more pressure on the little-toe side of the rear foot. If you have trouble initiating your turns, concentrate more pressure on the big-toe side of the front foot.

DROP YOUR REAR HEEL

In the beginning tele section you learned the telemark from a half wedge, a technique emphasizing the weight on the inside (rear) ski. In the tele, distributing more weight to the rear will result in better control of the last half of your turn. Your rear ski should bear at least half of your body weight—often more in certain kinds of snow. You can tell that you have enough weight back there when you feel the Achilles and calves of your rear leg stretch. You will automatically tuck

your hips under you to ease that tension.

For your next telemark turn go one step further. Relax your rear ankle so your heel drops closer to the ski. Stay on edge, of course, but try to get as much of your rear foot onto the ski as possible, as in the last illustration. The more foot you have on that back ski the more weight it gets, and the better you will be able to control it through the finish of each turn.

TIME YOUR EDGING

If you initiate your teles by stemming a front ski and *then* transferring weight to the rear ski, it is a two-step turn. Technicians call this a "sequential turn initiation" because the skis are edged in sequence. This "step telemark" is covered later in this book. It is one of those sequential turns used for moguls and hairy terrain. Its quick directional change allows you to "walk" down otherwise formidable slopes. But to effectively employ this turn you must have a

firm base to make a platform. Otherwise, you won't be able to step off the first ski and onto the second.

In deep snow I try to avoid stepping as much as possible. My reflexes aren't always quick enough to keep up with skis that are doing different things at different times. Here I prefer to edge my skis at the same time in a "simultaneous turn initiation." It's a bit more difficult but much more fluid and effective in working the skis. It carves them as opposed to turning them with one-two moves that employ stepping, steering, and skidding.

Try this fluid movement the next time you link teles. As you rise between turns, keep both skis flat during your lead change. Once the corrrect foot is forward for the new turn, edge both skis at the same time for the next turn. Pressure the skis under the big-toe side of your front foot and the little-toe side of your rear foot — *at exactly the same time*. Of course it's tempting to "feel" your way into a turn, stepping and edging first with your front ski. But don't forget that unequally edged skis often want to go off in different directions, making for some very uncomfortable positions. Simultaneous edging will result in a smoother, more advanced style of skiing. You won't need to feel your way into nearly as many soft snow conditions — you'll just jump in there and go for it.

DOING MORE WITH YOUR HIPS

An expert tele skier — from the waist up — will look very similar to an Alpine skier. His quiet upper body is always facing the next turn. But the radical differences between the leads of the two turns result in two very dissimilar postures from the waist down.

In Alpine skiing the pelvis faces more directly down the hill, with the uphill ski slightly ahead of the downhill one. A tele skier, however, must use his hips to effectively tip the skis onto their edges. The downhill ski is advanced, so the hips rotate with the

Edge both skis at the same time

turn rather than facing downhill. I think of it as "punching" my downhill hip around.

See in the illustration how the tele skier's hips punch through the turn, setting the skis on their edges and using the big hip muscles to keep them there. His upper body is "separated" from his lower body, facing quietly downhill as the skis arc back and forth.

When you use your hips to turn you *must* concentrate even more on facing your torso down the hill. When you make a turn the downhill hip rotates and your torso twists the other way. With skis and hips turning, nipples and navel always facing the fall line, your body acts as a coiled spring ready to be released. When you release your edges, those stretched back muscles and contracted stomach muscles whip your skis

into the next arc. Your turns become effortless, bomb-proof.

This is tele-anticipation, upper body and hands always facing the new turn. In this position I often feel my downhill (outside) hip bone digging into my ribs. It feels as though I could carry a pencil pinched between the lower rib cage and the crest of the hip bone.

A final note: make your stomach work as much as you can. The more you anticipate, especially with the tele's advanced outside hip, the more your stomach will work for you. If you feel your abdomen really getting a workout, then you are probably doing it right.

Use these ideas to refine your tele. And study "Skiing From the Waist Up" for more use of your upper body. In powder and crud, you'll be making graceful arcs while others auger.

Telemark anticipation

THE SELKIRKS

When I lived in southern British Colombia I was close to some of the best helicopter skiing in the world. I had always wanted to go heli-skiing, so I tried to get reservations for one of the single-day heli trips that was advertised at a very low price. I called the big outfits. Naively, I told them that my companion Jessie and I used three pins. A big mistake. None of these European-run operations would hear of having Nordic skiers in one of their groups. "What a bunch of Lugerheads!" I thought.

In a ski magazine I saw an advertisement for snow-cat skiing in the Purcell Range of the Selkirk Mountains — just south of the Bugaboos. It was cheap, and it wasn't far from my winter home. When I called no one seemed to mind what kind of skis we used. I confirmed the reservations. After two weeks of ski touring to quell some of the nervous anticipation, we rolled up to the quaint, out-of-the-way farmhouse run by our guides. It was spring, mud season.

The first morning we waded through the mud to the van that took us up the mountain to the cat garage. The snow cat, fully mired, was ready and waiting with at least twelve stereo speakers blaring. It was too noisy to talk, but I could tell Jessie and I were thinking the same thing — "It's too late now, can we keep up?"

Nice turn . . . Sean McNamara, skier
Photo by Ace Kvale

I hadn't been exposed to too many Alpine skiers. We went to ski areas, but three-pinners were very much the oddity. We usually stuck to ourselves. This Alpine group was diverse: two pairs of husbands and wives from Calgary, a couple of dope-smoking skiing buddies from Idaho, a retired paper-mill mogul from Michigan. It wasn't the hard-driving bunch of skiers that I would expect to find waiting for a throbbing helicopter.

The first run we skied was "Rolling Thunder." It was wide open, with about six inches of soft snow. I didn't turn, I just tried to hang on right behind the guide until we were down. I didn't want the free-heel skiers to be labeled the albatrosses of the bunch. My self consciousness didn't didn't last long. Once the guide fell, everyone relaxed.

The senior member of the group was the retired paper manufacturer. Don was his name. He said he was seventy. Don wore one of those suits that Canadian Mountain Holidays used to give away when a client had skied a million vertical feet. These days I think you can buy them, but not back then. Don was on his third free suit.

He was on his way to ski another hundred-thousand vertical with CMH, stopping off in the Selkirks for a week of low-pressure training. "Without practice, these old thighs just aren't what they used to be. I want to get another suit." Don had an old pair of Millers that he turned with ease. Ten years later, I still bump into Don in Vail on powder days. Not a bad life—I imagine he earned it.

We were the first three-pinners most of our Alpine companions had seen. Many of our runs were viewed as a performance. We hacked our way through every kind of snow, not always out of choice. I remember light so flat in an open bowl that we didn't know if we were going up or down. I also remember thinking I was going to throw up from vertigo. I watched our disoriented guide take a bad slammer in that flat light because of a sudden change in terrain. We skied through wind-deposited snow covering hard ice, breakable crust, and on the last day we skied in the rain—my first time.

And I remember carving turns in nice, heavy powder on the north side of the mountain, riding back up in the cat and skiing perfect corn on the sunny side. But it's the educational crud that comes to mind. From our guide I learned Alpine survival maneuvers that have lasted me through many a difficult snow condition. I learned how to choose where to turn. And I learned what those Lugerheads meant about Alpine skis and Alpine technique.

ADVANCED PARALLEL TIPS

Parallel turns are much more effective than telemarks on hard snow or in steep and narrow terrain. When you must face the fall line on a steep slope, the parallel turn's stance is stronger and more stable than the rotated position of the telemark. So even if it's not telemark dogma, to be as versatile as possible you can and should perfect your parallel turns.

Work on your basic parallel and accumulate some "mileage." Make enough parallel turns so that you can use them on any moderate terrain. Practice your stem christies, which are so useful when you need a very quick turn initiation. Once you've logged those miles, the next step is to develop your all-terrain parallel. You will want to make parallel turns in difficult conditions. You will want to make them instinctively.

To hone your turns we'll work on flexing your ankles, timing your edge change, directing your uphill knee, and feeling your edge under a certain part of your foot. These are all tricks that will transform your basic parallel turns into the arcs of an expert.

USING YOUR ANKLES

Alpine instructors always tell students to bend their knees. Knees, when flexed, act as shock absorbers. Bending them lowers your center of balance and increases your stability. Without knee bend you couldn't flex and extend your legs to weight and unweight your skis and control your edge pressure. Articulating your knees also facilitates angulation, both at the knee joints and at the hips.

Bend your knees, everyone.

But that's not the whole point of my focus. You must also bend your ankles. If you bend your knees and not your ankles you'll fall on your ass. More realistically, without flexible ankles your "shock absorbers" disappear. Your skis skid. With every little variation in the snow your weight goes to the extremes, either too far forward or too far back. You try to compensate, and your body

bends at the waist—that's the chicken-feeding stance.

Ankle bend is an important focus for Alpine skiers. It is difficult because most stiff Alpine boots don't bend freely. It's easy to spot an Alpine skier whose boots are too stiff: they are broken at the waist, clucking down the hill.

Ankle flex is much easier with bendable free-heel boots. It's not just for balance; the ankle joint, when flexed, becomes much more laterally stable. Flexing your ankles substitutes the human's biomechanics for an Alpine boot's plastic injection molding.

But alas, absence of boot stiffness means absence of support. In leather tele boots you can't just "prop" yourself up and rest against your cuffs. Sinking with your knees and ankles requires muscles to hold you there and to stand back up. Practice this exercise: relax in your athletic, rounded ski stance with stomach cupped, back relaxed, head up, eyes ahead. Push off down the slope and gain some momentum. Start with medium-radius, "skiddy" parallel turns, concentrating on smoothly flexing your *ankles* as you sink through each arc. In stiffer boots it helps to think about pulling up on your toes to get a good bend in your ankles. Extend your legs at the beginning of the turn, bending both of your ankles as the weight settles onto the *middle* of your outside foot. Avoid finishing the turns on your toes or heels. Try to feel your weight on your whole foot through the turn.

MAKING SMOOTHER TURNS

Rudimentary parallel turns are very abrupt and use lots of hard steering movements. Everything happens at once. But in all but the smoothest groomed snow conditions, free-heel skiers don't have the leverage to muster these exaggerated movements. Free-heel parallels have to be smooth, extra-efficient.

Free-heel skiers can pull off a smooth and elegant parallel turn by shifting

Flex your ankles

Shift to your outside ski earlier

their weight to the uphill ski earlier, *before* starting the next turn. Begin with a traverse, pushing off to gain a little speed. Now stand up tall and shift your weight to the uphill edge of your uphill ski. Once you have shifted weight to that uphill edge, *then* — no earlier! — tip the ski over into a turn, rolling it onto its inside edge. Voilà! It becomes your outside ski. Feel how your body seeks the fall line as you smoothly change edges and steer both skis into the turn.

Try it again. Sink through your last turn. As your skis come across the hill and your body finishes its sinking motion, immediately start the rise back up. Stand up tall; when your lower leg extends until it's almost straight, continue your upward movement by shifting to your uphill ski and edge. By shifting your weight to your uphill ski you'll be able to get even taller — your downhill ski actually will come up off of the snow. Once you're firmly shifted to that uphill ski's edge, *then* tip the ski over into a new turn, rolling it onto its inside edge. Focus your eyes down the hill and feel your body flow into the next turn.

Lead with your inside knee

YOUR INSIDE KNEE

For quick parallel turns, the inside ski is especially important. It must be *steered* and *edged* just like the outside one whether it is weighted or not. By focusing on your *inside knee*, you can fool your body into a better position for quicker, easier moves. Think of "leading" each new turn with your inside knee. It's like you were taking a hard corner on a bicycle, leaning into the turn with your knee. With that knee you point the inside ski's tip in the direction of the new turn. Simply steering with your inside ski will make your turns much quicker and easier.

EDGING YOUR INSIDE SKI

When you step or edge one ski at a time in loose snow your skis tend to wander off in different directions—especially with free heels. In fluff, semi-fluff, and crud you want to use *simultaneous* turning movements that move your two skis as one. Skis that are edged equally stay parallel even in heavy snow. You'll avoid many unplanned gymnastics brought about by crossed or diverging tips.

Make a series of turns and consciously focus on *edging* your inside ski. The inside ski doesn't need much weight for this edge to make a difference. Get used to the idea of edging the skis together and at the same time.

When in a deep-snow parallel you must also put weight on the inside edge. It's easiest for me to think about my feet: as my skis come into the fall line I like to feel weight on my inside foot. I pressure that foot under the bumpy part behind my little toe. Try it. Put enough weight on your inside foot to feel pressure behind the little toe.

The next time you're in deep snow, focus on these two-footed ideas. Maintain an aggressive attitude by moving continually down the hill. Be excited for each upcoming turn—try not to traverse the slope defensively. You will arc your two skis gracefully as one, seeking out the steep and deep.

KNEE-TO-BOOT CHASERS

"Knee-to-boot chasers" is an exercise I learned from a member of the PSIA Alpine Demonstration Team. They help you get your skis out to the side, away from your body, and up on their edges for more carving and less skidding. You don't need Alpine skis to do them; with free heels, knee-to-boot chasers will help you make a more technical turn. Skiing with your feet in

Knee-to-boot chasers

a hip-width stance, "chase" your inside
(uphill) boot with your outside (downhill) knee. Tip that inside boot away so
that the knee can't catch it. Notice
how your skis are tipped up on their
edges.

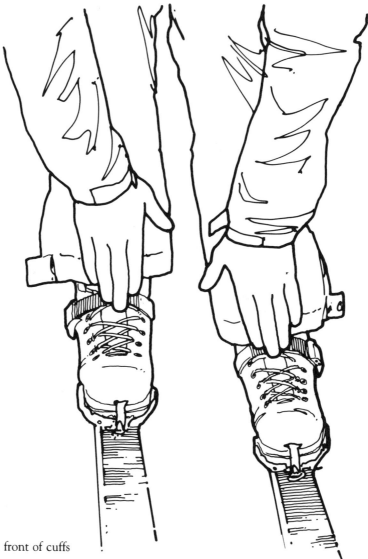

Hands in front of cuffs

Next try a similar idea with a different focus: move into the "inside corner" of your boot. As shown in the illustration, put your hands on the fronts of your boot cuffs. Now, think of your boots as though they have four corners. Move your hands to the inside (or uphill) corner of each boot, as shown in the next illustration. Press your shins toward your hands and toward the uphill corners. This inside corner is where you should press your shins as you move into each new turn.

Now make a series of turns, consciously initiating each by pressing into both inside *corners*—don't press straight forward. Stick with the corners all the way through the turn. Your body should move gracefully into the fall line, the skis well-edged throughout the arc.

DRIVING YOUR HEELS

Try a completely different focus: your heels. This is an idea that will get more

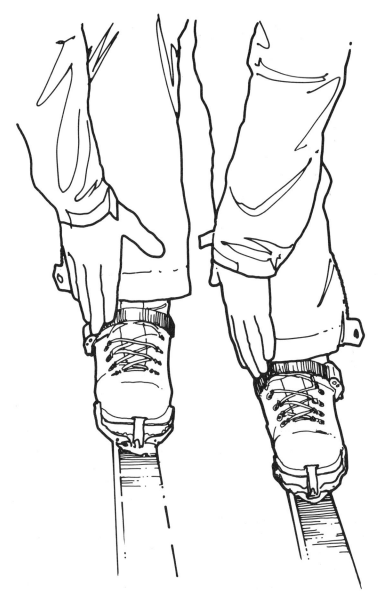

Hands on "inside corners"
—where you apply pressure
on the boot cuff

rebound and snap from advanced turns. Since your heels aren't fastened down, it also helps keep your balance centered in a stable position to reduce the chance of a forward fall.

Carve a few smooth arcs, feeling the weight on your whole outside foot throughout the turn. Now change your focus and think about the heel of your foot. As you round the bend and your skis come out of the fall line, *drive your heels* toward the finish of the arc. That's right, try to push your heels ahead. Don't sit back. Just think heels, weighting your feet from the arch backward.

These movements don't merely emphazise your feet and legs. By focusing on specific lower-body movements and sensations, your upper body wants to move in the right direction—in the direction of the next turn. You'll soon find yourself seeking the fall line with your torso and skiing more aggressively. Your turns will become indistinguishable from those of a strong Alpine skier.

SKIING FROM THE WAIST UP

A few winters ago Yvon Chouinard and I travelled to Japan to ski on the island of Hokkaido. What a place to ski! Hokkaido was enjoying its usual bumper winter with an abundance of cold, fresh powder. We toured all over the island, chauffered by a stately, elderly Japanese friend who would sneak away to soak in the nearby hot springs while we beat ourselves up on the slopes.

It's rare when recreational skiers in Japan venture off the piste. At the top of each lift only a short walk would bring us to acres of virgin snow. The best slopes were serviced by odd little single chairs—the Japanese are very private people. In a chair no larger than a dinner plate for my American-sized seat, I clung to the bar looking for more untouched terrain and those perfectly spaced Japanese trees. We climbed nearby peaks, we night-skiied, we soaked sore muscles in blistering-hot baths.

I remember well an out-of-the-way little spot at the large Niseko ski area; a gully with heavy, deep snow topped with a desperate wind crust. It was difficult. If you hesitated the least bit between turns your skis wouldn't come around. Both Yvon and I became possessed with the idea of skiing this crud, caught up in the aggressive attitude it demanded. You had to plant your pole as firmly as the snow allowed and *totally* commit your upper body down the hill. A loud grunt was the perfect signal to begin each new arc.

Typically austere, our Japanese ski partners didn't know what to think about the two Americans fanatically grunting down the desperate slope, riding up on the dinner plate, and going back again. They would follow us politely, quietly face-planting in the treacherous conditions. But finally even Japanese patience succumbed; exasperated, they tried it, first grunting tentatively, then aggressively, as they committed their bodies to the fall line and their turning efforts began to work.

ANTICIPATION

Commitment. It's not easy facing down the hill on a steep slope, but you must. The attitude is called "anticipation." It was named by the French skier Georges Joubert in reference to the torso's positioning in anticipation of the upcoming turn. Learn it well. It's an important key to all advanced skiing.

Anticipation isn't so simple as "facing down the hill" or "not moving your upper body." Or thinking about the next turn. These are just instructor's clichés—we're all guilty of using them. Advanced anticipation requires proper poling, separation of the upper and lower body, dynamic movement of the torso into the fall line—all focuses that will change you from a good skier into a great one. By facing in the right direction, your skiing will become easier, more effective, and more elegant.

Anticipation has to be developed by degrees. For the beginner it starts with the eyes, taking them off the ski tips to look farther down the hill. For the intermediate it's pointing chest and hands down the hill. For the advanced skier it's incorporating pole plants to "block" the torso and face the arms and shoulders down the hill. For the expert, it's movement. It's an attitude of the upper body that, when combined with momentum, becomes total freedom—an independent upper body confidently floating toward the next turn while the skis turn freely back and forth. The torso moves independent of the legs as though it were joined only by a ball-and-socket or universal joint.

To achieve this freedom the expert skier combines *all* of the basic points of anticipation. He uses his eyes, torso, arms, shoulders, and pole plants together. Each one of these elements is important from the beginning. Experts always go back to them. They use them as a way to cure bad habits or just as a way to relax for a difficult descent.

Tele anticipation

Sometimes I think of my shoulders as an articificial horizon on an instrument panel of an airplane. I try to keep that artificial horizon level with the horizon of the snowslope.

You can also think of your navel as though it has a string running from it. As you link your turns, imagine someone pulling you down the hill with that string. Let the string pull you; don't pull against it. The feeling, the focus, is *weightlessness* as you allow gravity's string to pull you down the fall line. Think of your nipples as headlights. Pick a target down the hill in the fall line and shine your high beams at it.

As you make turns, keep your lights on the target without veering.

Thinking is great, but you also need concrete, instinctive technique—poling technique.

POLING

Back in the old days skiers used one pole like an outrigger, leaning on it for balance and dragging it between their legs as a brake. It must have been hard to ski with a quiet upper body while swinging a big stick. Today's poling technique is altogether different. Two

Arms too high— "Mammy" turns

poles are used both for timing your turns and for positioning your upper body. Your skis do the braking.

To employ two-pole technique your poles must be the right length. For downhill skiing, whether Alpine or telemark, Alpine-length poles are the best choice. When touring, your poles should be longer for forward purchase on uphills and flats.

So what do you do in the backcountry, where the terrain goes both up and down? Many skiers adapt their downhill technique to long Nordic poles by holding their arms very high,

Al Jolson style. "Mammy turns," I call them. Other skiers choke up on their long poles as though they were baseball bats. These are both compromises. If you hold your poles high in the air your body tips backwards, making quick turns very difficult. You feel as though you are "spinning out" at the finish of each turn. If you choke up on your poles, you lose your grip. On very steep slopes a firm pole plant is most important—you *must* have a good grip.

An excellent solution for backcountry skiing is a pair of adjustable poles that telescope from Alpine to

Nordic touring length. You can adjust them long on the flats and uphills, short on the downhills, and two different lengths on long traverses.

POLES FOR BALANCE

Once you get your pole length straightened out there are specific poling exercises for improving your technique. You can eliminate your dependence on poles for balance and learn to employ them primarily for timing and body position.

Here is an old Alpine exercise especially useful for tele skiers who depend on their poles for balance: hold your poles horizontally across your body. You will have in each hand the grip of one pole and the shaft of the other. Hold them with your arms relaxed in front of your chest. Try to keep the

Cross your body with your poles

poles level with your shoulders. Think of the poles as a carpenter's level, and try to keep the middle bubble even with the snow's horizon.

Removing the crutch of your poles can make you painfully conscious of bad habits. For instance, many telemark skiers have a habit of leaning on their uphill pole. They use a rapid uphill pole plant for balance at the finish of each turn and for propulsion into the next. Once that pole is gone their pole-check becomes a butt-check. If you feel that without your poles you are falling uphill too much, put more weight on your back foot in the little-toe area at each turn's finish.

Once you feel comfortable linking tele or parallel turns without poles, you can let your poles drop to a normal position. Keep your hands in the same spot as when holding your poles across your body — within your peripheral vision. You don't need to plant the poles, simply find a comfortable position for your hands, poles pointing behind you.

POLES FOR TIMING

Poles are put to good use by timing your turns. A proper pole plant stores energy and regulates the release of that energy into the next turn. Practice turn timing. Tap the snow lightly with the downhill pole before you start each turn. Then turn your skis around the hole you've made in the snow. Think tap, turn. Tap, turn. Tap, turn. Plant only the downhill pole for each new turn. Planting the downhill (inside) pole may be contrary to telemark dogma, but either double poling or planting only the uphill pole will reinforce the bad habits I mentioned earlier.

Uphill pole plants lean and rotate your body uphill into the slope — the wrong way to be facing. Double pole plants are used by some skiers for security in that unstable transition between turns. But this habit squares the body on the skis so that quick turning requires propulsion off the two planted poles — a difficult feat in soft snow.

Remember when practicing your poling that it requires timing — an elu-

Pole plant as you rise — a gentle tap

sive skill of feel and image rather than of conscious thought. If you get confused while practicing this skill think about something else. Watch good Alpine skiers and imitate their poling movements. Follow a good skier, planting your pole in the same spots that he plants his and turning your skis in the same tracks. Don't think, try to see and feel.

DIFFERENT POLING FOR DIFFERENT TURNS

Watch any good Alpine skier and you will notice that his hands stay comfortable and controlled. Hands help create the right attitude for the rest of the body. Hold your arms comfortably

flexed, not outstretched, keeping your hands in front of you in the periphery of your vision.

When cruising and making larger-radius turns, a pole plant is used primarily to position your body and signal the edge change for the next turn. There is a relaxed, flowing transition between turns. A gentle pole plant is used as you *rise up* into the new arc. With these big turns you're probably skiing fast, so the pole plant should be a gentle tap, not a firm sting that might slow you down.

In some higher-speed Giant Slalom-type turns this tap becomes so gentle it's nonexistent, an imagined pole plant to "set you up." When watching

The short-radius pole plant
is an aggressive *sting*

World Cup Giant Slalom competitions I have often noticed this minimal pole plant. Those skiers are so skilled, however, that they can assume an aggressive upper body attitude without the need of a pole plant to orient their torso. I prefer a gentle pole plant over none at all.

In short-radius turns, especially on steeper terrain, you want to decelerate, not accelerate. Applied in the split-second transition between quick turns, the pole plant becomes a braking technique. It is firm and decisive at the final *downward* movement of your body as you finish the turn and begin the next. It's a *sting*. I think of it as simultaneously stinging the snow with my edges and my downhill pole before moving into the new turn.

Your pole plant sets you up for short-radius turns. It's a move crucial to making the skis come around easily in otherwise difficult snow. Plant your pole with the basket advanced. The planted pole pushes back against your arm and shoulder and forces your upper body to face downhill. The body twist created by this "blocking" movement stores energy in contracted and stretched muscle groups. When you release this energy into the next turn your skis are launched into the arc with minimal effort.

The pole plant "opens the door" down the hill

Think of your poling as though you are opening a door for your torso to move through. The door opens into the next turn. In short turns, that means the door opens directly down the hill, in longer turns, across the hill.

For some skiers, thinking of *where* to plant the pole is easier. Notice where the pole is planted in the short-radius turns in the last illustration. The skier's pole is planted clear back by the heel of the boot. This helps frame the door for the next turn. Plant the pole farther back toward the heel for short turns, farther ahead toward the ski tip for longer turns.

A different idea will help prevent your hands from dropping behind, a common error that leans you into the hill. Once you plant your pole focus on punching the poling hand forward and "over" the pole. On steeps, exaggerate this idea, punching your hand down the hill. Resist the temptation to let it fall behind; keep your hand moving down the fall line.

POLING IN CRUD
Subtle hand movements can work wonders to bring your skis around in thick conditions. I mentioned earlier that the inside hand on the planted pole

Raise your outside hand up and forward as you plant your pole

moves forward, over the pole. The outside (uphill) hand will also aid your turning—especially in difficult snow.

Try it in crud: as you move aggressively into a telemark or parallel turn, throw your outside hand sharply up and forward, down the hill. See in the illustration how the inside pole is planted while the outside hand is moving up and forward.

Inside hand, outside hand—you can't think about it all at once. As I mentioned before, when you get confused, don't think about anything. Poling is predominately a matter of tim-

ing, a technique that is easier to ape than describe. Find that good Alpine skier and mimic his moves.

FOLLOW THE FALL LINE

Momentum. Flowing with gravity. That's the sign of a true expert, the skier who seems to move effortlessly down the steepest slopes in perfect control.

Appearances can be deceiving. Watch a really good skier making short turns down some steep, narrow path and it will look as though his upper body is completely "quiet," motionless. It's no wonder that instructors teach and students construe the torso's attitude as a position. It's so calm it looks almost static. But don't be fooled by that steadfast appearance. The torso is moving aggressively toward the next turn. The trunk isn't following the legs, it's leading, moving down the hill in a much straighter line than the skis. It is not rotating side to side.

This concept is a much more advanced form of "anticipation." The point is, this anticipation isn't just a static position "facing" down the hill. It's dynamic, and fluid. Notice how, in the illustration, the upper body follows a much straighter line than that of the skis. This line varies according to your turn radius just as the track that your skis follow does. Usually, the tighter the turn radius, the straighter the line your body will take. In short-radius turns there's simply no time for your heavy torso to follow the serpentine path of your skis.

Following such a line with the torso requires aggressive movement down the hill. While your skis are snaking back and forth under that "floating" trunk, your stomach, back, and buttocks are stretching and contracting, storing and releasing energy into each successive turn. It's a workout. There's nothing "quiet" or static about it.

Try it, moving your torso into each new turn sooner while your skis are finishing the last turn. It's a very dynamic feeling as your skis race in one direction across the hill while you commit your upper body to the opposite direction, into the *next* turn. Use your practice slope: as your skis come across the

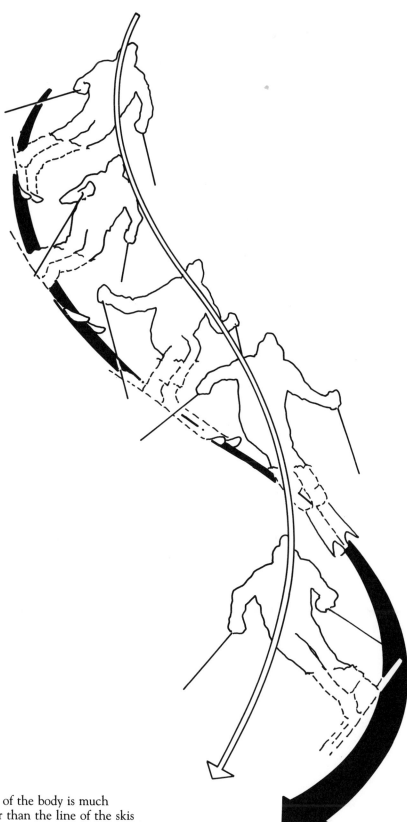

The line of the body is much
straighter than the line of the skis

Move toward the new turn
as you plant your pole

slope toward the finish of a turn, plant your downhill pole and move your whole torso toward a new one. Your skis will go one way while your upper body moves the other. It seems unlikely, but your skis miraculously snap around, finishing the last turn crisply and rebounding toward the new one.

When telemarking with this focus you'll develop a "wind-up" effect, twisting the body like a spring, storing energy to release and snap you into the next turn. In parallel turns you will feel your weight shift to the uphill ski before it's steered into a new turn.

Parallel or telemark, this fluid movement preserves the momentum of the upper body rather than slowing it. It goes hand-in-hand with the telemark christy. For me, it's one of the most elegant sensations of descent on skis, the flowing with gravity.

MOUNT SOPRIS

We staggered up the talus field in pitch darkness, armed with one very weak and another completely broken headlamp. I must have suffered a memory lapse when I agreed to do this two days in a row. Yesterday we had done the same thing on Mount Daly, stumbling off into the dark with an Alpine start. At least yesterday there was a road and a moon. And a great descent.

Two hours later it was as though the talus had never existed. We had other things to worry about as we whacked our way up a near-ice slope.

We finally reached the summit with toes smashed from kicking steps. There was a change in plan; no way were we going to ski the slope we had just ascended. It was a shady sheet of ice.

The other side, in the sun, looked beautiful. It was a vast, open bowl. We relaxed and enjoyed a thermos of tea. I was first to descend, so I felt I shouldn't break protocol to stop to rest my aching thighs. My turns got bigger and bigger—fortunately the snow was forgiving. That first bowl was the longest, but there was more: little steep shots, trees, meadows— six thousand feet in all.

Back at the car, it took us an hour or so to get out of the mud. I knew we carried those shovels for something. Two switchbacks down the old road, stopping to look back, we spotted another line.

"Hey Michael, do you have to work tomorrow? Maybe we should give that slope a try."

Another memory lapse.

The author spring-skiing
Photo by Michael Kennedy

115

TRAINING FOR BACKCOUNTRY SKIING

The best training for skiing is skiing, but we all don't have the luxury of skiing year around. Besides, you need to participate in exercise other than skiing to develop the muscles that aren't so important to turns but that just might stave off fatigue and injury while skiing. The first criterion for any kind of training is to choose a form of exercise that you enjoy enough to maintain. If you don't like it, you probably won't do it.

Another criterion—one to be approached prudently—is specificity: if you have to make maximum use of a limited amount of training time, muscle-specific exercises will produce the greatest benefit. World-class coaches emphasize this training specificity to the extreme because they want their athletes to make the most of every training minute. Cross-country racers, for example, don't just go running— they always run with ski poles. To me this idea is a bit too much like work and is a good way to ruin a perfectly enjoyable run. I try to choose an exercise first because it's fun, second because it's applicable to skiing.

Stretching before a workout is a great psyche-up and helps to prevent muscle injury. You don't need Jane Fonda, Richard Simmons, or sitar music in the background—just a few stretches that are muscle specific to your sport. It helps to read up on the subject—Bob Anderson's *Stretching* is an excellent primer. Always start with an easy warmup before you stretch. This is crucial, since cold muscles don't stretch—they tear. Start easy to get your pulse up and your blood moving. Warm down in the same way, slowing to relax your muscles. Don't cool off too quickly. I often do extended post workout warm-downs in front of the TV, although there is a danger of losing a few brain cells.

The more you exercise, the more important it is to rest. Organize your schedule to include both hard and easy days for maximum benefit from your training. Alternate the hard and easy days, and take one complete rest day each week. Otherwise you will become tired and "overtrained." You will rarely be rested enough to push yourself to get the most from each workout.

How long should you train each day? You don't have to maintain a rigid schedule to get plenty of positive benefit from training, but some guidelines are helpful. Using a "normal" week as an example, I train about an hour each work day and reserve a long, easy workout for Saturday (two to three hours) and a long, hard day on Sunday (one and a half to two and a half hours). Monday is for resting. Climbing or skiing over the weekend counts toward the long workout—isn't that what you're training for? Monday's rest is certainly crucial to healing over-exerted muscles, but I find it even more important for keeping up my interest. Take a day off and you'll be more excited about getting rolling the next day.

It is important to monitor your body during each workout, otherwise you might push harder than you should for a slow "recovery" workout and compromise the next hard one. Or you might coast through a hard workout and not gain the maximum benefit from it. By checking your pulse rate you can accurately monitor each day's training. Your pulse is the "tachometer" of a workout. It indicates how hard you are pushing your body.

To determine your actual pulse rate during a workout, stop and count your heartbeats for fifteen seconds and multiply that number by four. If you don't want to stop, you can use a pulsemeter. I use one with a wireless sending unit that straps around the chest and a wristwatch that displays my pulse rate. The figure you get from your calculations or pulsemeter should fall within your "training range." If your pulse is too low you should speed up. If it's too high, ease off a bit.

To estimate your "training range" first determine your maximum pulse rate by subtracting your age from 225. Your training range should fall between seventy percent and eighty percent of the maximum rate. If you are thirty-two for example, your maximum pulse rate is 193 beats per minute and should range between 132 and 155 during training. Note that this is a rough guideline that varies according to your fitness and the altitude.

On easy days, don't exceed the lower end of your training range, around seventy percent of your maximum. Concentrate on keeping your pulse down because you want your body to rest for the harder workouts. On hard days stay closer to the eighty percent mark, which will mean that your body is approaching its anaerobic threshold: the stage at which you get "pumped." These hard days require the most recovery time.

Once you have a good aerobic base, you can increase your speed through specific training: alternately crossing and retreating from your "anaerobic threshold." With this kind of training your body will grow accustomed to a higher energy output and greater speed. A spontaneous sort of speed training

that I enjoy is called *fartlek*, a Swedish term for speed play. During *fartlek* you increase your speed at random and slow the pace for recovery when you tire. For instance, when on my bicycle, on a course with rolling hills I jam the on ups and rest on the downs.

A more regimented kind of speed training is "intervals." When doing intervals you closely monitor alternating periods of high-energy output and recovery. With anaerobic intervals you extend yourself past your eighty percent mark for a short time (usually between thirty seconds and three minutes), then slow for recovery until your pulse drops to one hundred beats. Time the recovery period: when it takes markedly longer than the first interval for your pulse to drop, you have done enough intervals.

For intervals—and any kind of speed training—it is important to be well rested and have a good training base. Warm up, stretch, and warm down. Start off with very short intervals, and don't push too hard. Too little speed

How "Speed" Miller got his name
Photo by Ace Kvale

training won't do you any harm—it is too much speed training that injures many athletes. Consult a good running book like *The Complete Book of Running* or Marty Hall's *One Stride Ahead* to set up a speed-training schedule.

SKATING

The evolution from classical cross-country technique to skating has done more to improve my downhill skiing than any other activity. The movements for snow skating are easy to duplicate on pavement. Its not only fun but it's muscle-specific for downhill as well as cross-country ski training. Skates with in-line wheels or roller skis

designed for skating are your best choice for skate training. Add long cross-country skating poles and you will effectively train your upper as well as your lower body. There are several good books on skating available. And find a smooth pavement—you will feel every bump on those tiny wheels.

STRENGTH TRAINING

I keep trying to convince my girlfriend that aerobic athletes must be scrawny to be good—especially when she's gawking at my buddies' biceps and thighs. It's true that skiers need strength for leg-pumping crud, packing a big load into a backcountry cabin, or squeezing off that last desperate turn. Most important, specific-strength training makes a skier more resistant to injury. Pushups, situps (the abdomen is especially important to skiers), pullups and all sorts of calesthenics are simple, effective strength-builders.

It usually takes some kind of toy or apparatus to keep me interested in strength training my legs. Nautilus is a great workout, but it isn't always available and is not very portable. For maximum portability there are several stretch devices for strength and flexibility training. These are tools that, when attached to a fixed object, can be pulled in different directions to exercise specific muscles.

My favorite of these is the Sport Cord. It was introduced to me by U.S. Ski Team Trainer John Atkins as part of my recuperative program after knee surgery. A very simple, portable training device, the Sport Cord was developed for elite athletes' specific-strength training and is used both as a preventative against injury and as part of a recuperative program after injury. It's a great workout.

Regardless of your choice of exercise, keeping yourself excited about being fit is the key to success. Choose training activities that are fun, like skating and cycling, those that exercise the right muscle groups for skiing. Rest to preserve your enthusiasm for each session and alternate the difficulty of various sessions. You will find yourself more fit and your skiing more fun and enjoyable.

4
FREE-HEELING IN POWDER, CRUD, AND MOGULS

POWDER

Slow-motion grace, effortless movement. Cold, light snow bubbling over my head and pressing sensuously against my body. That's what I feel when I hear the word "powder."

The locals wait for it. Tentative skiers avoid it. No, it isn't effortless, but it's ultimate. Powder skiing *demands* proper technique. The snow changes frequently from turn to turn. It weighs heavily on your skis when the sun beats down. It grows dense and perilous with pounding wind.

The resistance of powder snow can give you a false sense of security. You feel as though you don't have to finish your turns because the snow slows you down. But you'll find that as the terrain steepens you'd better finish your turns round and controlled or you're quickly out of control. And unlike skiing on a groomed slope, you can't simply steer your skis sideways to scrape off speed, unless you want to head plant. You must control your speed with the arc of your turn, flexing your skis from the very start to the very finish of each one. Learn to turn your skis in round, complete arcs and you'll have the technique for the ultimate powder runs, the real steep and deep.

Most skiers have so little opportunity to ski powder that it takes them years to learn how. Unless you live at one of a handful of the legendary deep-snow areas, there is too little of it for consistent practice. There are, however, a number of exercises that, with practice, will help you hone your powder skiing as quickly as possible. These ideas apply to both parallel and telemark skiers.

You need to get the feel of equal-weight distribution between your skis. And equal edging. You want to utilize your entire range of motion, with a strong emphasis on extension and flexion of the legs. And there's the ultimate move that is a key to expert powder skiing: aggressively moving your body down the hill toward the next turn.

I'll start with the first idea. It's worth noting for this practice that even if you are an expert piste skier it's best when

practicing powder technique to stay clear of rocks and trees. Find a gentle, open slope, ideally one that is covered with a blanket of light, fresh snow. Start by practicing straight running. Once you build a little speed, shift your weight from one ski to the other. Quickly you will feel how weight is best distributed between your feet: evenly. It's not like the light-inside-foot, weight-on-the-outside-foot rule for packed slopes. Make some straight runs in the flats and get the feeling of this equal distribution.

Now, still without turning, start moving up and down. You can practice this with your feet in a parallel position or by switching tele leads if you're working on your teles. You should employ a bouncing rhythm, standing tall and sinking, extending and flexing. If you're tele skiing think of sinking *between* your feet. This is a good way to start any powder run, feeling the snow for its resistance and consistency.

Are you comfortable with your weight distribution? Then try a turn: while rising (tele or parallel), press hard on your feet and twist them into a turn. Some describe this as grinding their heels into the turn. Rise with your body, pressing as you twist your feet, grinding your heels into the cold, light snow. It's easiest to practice one turn at a time, turning into the hill to a stop. Can you feel how your skis flex into an arc, scribing a turn?

Note the difference in your footwork between parallels and teles: if you are in a parallel stance you're pushing both of your heels away from you evenly. In a telemark you're grinding on the heel of your front foot and on the *little toe* of the rear foot. For telemark skiers the rear ski is crucial, so be conscious of exerting plenty of weight on that back ski.

To link your turns you will have to add the other "half" to the extension of your legs: a flexion, a sinking motion, relaxing and contracting your legs as you finish each turn. It makes sense. Without sinking, you can't rise again into another arc. Extension and flexion

Exaggerate flexion and
extension in powder

is the distinctive up-and-down technique you see in the films, skiers elegantly using both ends of their range of motion, high and low.

Rise sharply and press your feet away from you to initiate either a telemark or a parallel turn. As your skis come out of the fall line sink and twist your feet into the turn finish. You won't have to try very hard. The resistance of the snow will help finish your turn, pulling your skis further around as you twist your feet, pushing them up and flexing your legs as the pressure builds under your skis. Don't resist; relax your legs as this pressure builds, letting the snow do the work for you. This automatic flexion, and letting the snow do the pushing, is why powder skiers call their favorite turns "effortless."

Gain some speed on your gentle slope, rising and pressing with your feet to start the turns, sinking as you turn your feet into the finish. When you feel the bouncy rhythm add a pole plant at the lowest point of each bounce. This will punctuate each turn,

setting you up for a rise into your next one.

So what about the steep and deep we hear so much about? There are tricks for teles or parallel turns that you should always keep available:

Reread the last item about rhythm and bounce. Try to see that up-and-down rhythm in your mind's eye. Watch Warren Miller movies, ski-school videos, cable TV, and good skiers under the lift. Use any visual trick that gives you an image of that loose, bouncy rhythm.

Face down the hill. I know I've said it many times, but you really need to do it here. Face those arms, nipples, and navel right down the hill as though you're perfectly confident your turns will happen. Telemark skiers have to exaggerate this body twist because it's much harder to face the fall line with the rotated hip of the telemark movement. Exaggerate your up-and-down movement. Stand taller and sink lower than you think is possible. Rise sharply to emphasize the "pressing away" of

your feet, flexing your skis as soon as you begin the arc. Sharply raise your outside hand up and forward as you rise in order to emphasize your body's extension. Practice garlands on steeper slopes, turning into the hill to a stop.

The crux on the steeps certainly isn't turning into the hill to a stop. It's turning into the fall line. This time, link some turns. As your skis come out of the fall line and you feel the resistance of the snow slowing you down, relax your legs. Let the snow push your feet up into the turn finish. The powder's resistance will help you sink through the turn and push your feet upward to "automatically" flex your legs.

As the snow pushes your skis up and around, it packs into a platform under your feet. Reach down the fall line and plant your pole to signal the next turn. Now you're committed. Keeping your legs relaxed, "roll" (for parallel turns) your skis off the platform and into the next turn. Rather than rolling off the platform, tele skiers should shuffle the inside foot forward off the platform and into a new lead. As your skis roll or shuffle toward the fall line, move your body aggressively into the next turn: extend your legs, rise sharply, and raise your outside hand to emphasize the extension.

As your skis drop off the platform they'll be very light. Try to make them heavier with your extension and bend them into an arc. Think about keeping them deep in the snow. "Reach" down the hill with your feet. You'll know it the moment you feel it — that weightlessness as your skis drop off the platform and your body's complete extension as your feet reach for the snow below.

A bad habit to break is sitting back. Once you do that it's too easy to get stuck there in the "back seat." You simply don't have to sit back in powder in order to keep your tips up. In parallel turns I like to emphasize the weight on the rear two-thirds of my foot from the arch back. In tele turning I emphasize the weight *between* my feet, with plenty of rear-foot pressure. When you want

to get a turn around more quickly, press on your toes (for a parallel) or your front foot (for a telemark) from this centered position without committing your body too far forward. Just stand centered and press down on your toes, or front ski, to get the tips turning.

Just as important as fore-to-aft weight distribution in powder is your weight distribution from side-to-side. In deep snow parallel skiers *weight* and *edge* both skis much more evenly than on packed slopes. Many refer to this equal weighting as "skiing two skis as one." Telemark skiers weight and edge both skis, too, with plenty of weight on the rear ski, arcing their telemarks as though they are on one long ski. If you don't weight and edge both skis you will have all sorts of problems: the

splits, crossed tips, or high-speed figure-elevens. If you step your turns around you'll have similar troubles. Beware. You must weight *and* edge both of your skis simultaneously as you initiate each turn. Avoid stem christies, step teles, or any "one-two" type turns.

Notice how I keep talking about parallel turns. Yes, free-heel parallels are possible in powder. Sure, it's intimidating to try to turn in deep snow without sticking that leading ski ahead for security. But if you want to practice parallels, just find good powder that's not too deep or grabby. Try to make as many parallel turns as you can, and when you get in trouble drop into a tele. You'll soon find that you won't have to make that survival tele. You'll be looking for opportunities to powder parallel.

Edge both skis equally, whether making telemark or parallel turns

A good exercise to review if you're working on parallel turns is one found in the "Advanced Free-Heel Techniques." It helps you edge both skis equally with parallels. (You might think of it as tipping over the skis since you really aren't edging into a hard surface.) As you tip (edge) your skis into each new turn, focus on pointing your inside knee in this new turning direction.

Telemarkers can weight both skis evenly by emphasizing pressure on the back foot. Tuck your rear leg snugly under you. Don't let it trail behind. Be

Think big toe, little toe

sure to edge both skis simultaneously, moving onto the little toe of your rear foot at the same time you pressure the big toe of your front foot. Yeah, it's "big-toe, little-toe" again. It will help to go back to the advanced telemark section to review these ideas.

Once you're more comfortable with the idea of powder and getting your skis around in it, work on your anticipation. As I said before, it's not just a static facing of the torso down the hill but a dynamic movement of the body into the next turn. At first it's hard to make this aggressive move in powder. Your natural reaction is to rotate defensively, keeping your upper body in the *last* turn rather than moving it into the

next one. It feels secure. But what have you got to lose? The snow's soft, and it's easy to stop.

Try it. Find a slope with soft, forgiving snow, tighten your cuffs and zippers, put on your hat, and go for it. Make yourself move your body into the next turn. The emphasis I used in "Skiing from the Waist Up" was, as your skis come across the hill to finish the last turn, move your upper body in the *opposite* direction. Keep trying and you'll feel it.

Ah, that weightless feeling of moving your body confidently down the hill toward the fall line. Once you experience that sensation you will have opened the door to truly expert skiing.

CHRISTMAS, 1983

It was Christmas Day. If you were there, you would remember. It had snowed every day for the last forty days. That morning there were nineteen inches of new snow, rounding out the accumulated snowfall of the last thirty-six hours to thirty-two inches. And the road from Denver as well as the Denver airport were closed. We had the mountains to ourselves.

Christmas with no customers. How often does that happen? Not that I wished it; as a ski instructor, I needed the tourists to make a living. And the ski area had to stay alive. But if the snow's there, you had better ski it because it won't last long.

It looked as though the ski school and patrol would get along without us, so several of my old college buddies and I convened for a little Christmas celebration at the bottom of the upper lift. My best friend, Chuck, a ski patroller, had been trying to get a new part of the mountain open to the public. We had skied it numerous times in the past — the Peak, it was called — but it had been closed to all but the ski patrol and those few friends whom the patrol allowed to tag along quietly. But the next day it would be open to the public.

Climbing it required a short hike from the top of the new lift. There was so much snow on top you had to clear out a spot to put your skis on. It went up your

Craig Hesse contemplates
his next turn
Photo by Ace Kvale

nose when you bent over. I tightened my scarf around my mouth, thinking I'd need it to breathe. Darlene went first — after all, it was Christmas. It would be my turn next.

God, I hate that first turn, when everyone watches. Even after years of teaching I hate it. I always over-turn, over-compensate, over-something. Miraculously, I made it through the first two turns and realized what I was in for. I had never skied snow like this in Colorado — a Utah-deep dump of dry snow on steep terrain.

With every turn I had that wonderful gurgling sound of light snow pummeling my goggles. I leaned my torso precariously against the snow's depth, exaggerating movements to get my slow-motion turns around. The deluge of snow quickly packed my goggles — I couldn't see at all. But I didn't want to raise a hand to clear them and break my rhythm. Darlene was happily squealing, so I blindly made my way toward the sound, arcing the tightest turns I could muster until I came to a stop.

MORE FREE-HEEL TURNS

Motion is what makes your skis go round. Vertical movements lighten and pressure your skis at the proper moment in each arc to get the most from your skis for as little effort as possible.

The low, bent-kneed position of the "classic" telemark has influenced many free-heel skiers to stay locked in a genuflecting position throughout their tele turns—or stuck in a crouch in parallel turns. "Locked" is the word— there is little maneuverability once down there, and crouching low often results in a pair of sore knees. A too-low position causes more than knee strain, though. Bruised and broken patellas are common among low-flying telemarkers whose rear knees skim the snow. Trolling with your kneecaps is a good way to find stumps and rocks.

If you learn to contract and extend your legs, what was once a static, too-low position gives way to a fluid up-and-down movement. In parallel or telemark turning you need this flexion and extension to control the pressure that builds as your skis come across the fall line. Up-and-down movement smooths out your turns. Without it turning is jerky, imprecise, and skiddy with uncontrolled chatter. But when you compensate for increased pressure with vertical motion your skis glide and edge smoothly. They turn freely, carving like a knife.

Your skis are most likely to skid at the finish of each turn as they come across the hill. Once across the fall line they resist the force of gravity that is pulling your body downhill and increasing the pressure against your edges. If you do not lighten your skis to absorb this excess pressure they will begin to "chatter."

On hard snow we instinctively want to stiffen and straighten our legs to resist chatter, but the best thing to do is to lighten the skis by sinking and compensating for the pressure increase. In order to have the necessary range of

motion to make this movement you
should be tall early in the turn—otherwise you will have no where to sink.

NOW TURNS

There is a great skiing exercise called
the "now" turn (some call it the "patience" turn) to emphasize this feeling
of up-and-down motion. I was first
taught this exercise by Walt Chauner,
a member of the PSIA Alpine Demonstration Team. I have since used it suc-
cessfully with many free-heel students
with unanimous results. These students
improved their turning rhythm, their
maneuverability, and their pressure
control on their edges. The now turn
emphasizes a tall, extended position by
delaying the sinking motion until the
skis are directly in the fall line.

Find a wide, moderate slope. Using
either parallel- or telemark-turning
technique, stand very tall, as shown in
the first illustration. Stay in this tall

position until you reach NOW, as
shown in the second illustration. Don't
sink until your skis are pointing directly
down the hill. Say "now" out loud, and
sink into the turn finish once your skis
are in the fall line. When sinking be
sure that you flex at the ankles and
knees, not at the waist.

Link a sequence of now turns down
the hill, concentrating on first standing
tall, then delaying the sinking motion.
You will notice that the extension-con-
traction of your legs creates more
rhythm in your skiing. Feel how
smoothly and crisply your skis finish
each turn as the sinking lightens the
pressure on your edges and tightens
your turn finish. At first the up-and-
down motion might feel exaggerated,
but you'll soon find that it makes your
skis snap around more smoothly and
quickly.

Whether you parallel or telemark,
the elements are the same. Don't throw
out your low position. Ski "through" it

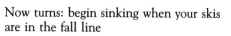

Now turns: begin sinking when your skis
are in the fall line

with a dynamic, rhythmic up-and-down motion.

THE TELEMARK TWO-STEP

The step telemark is a great technique for quick turns on radically steep and bumpy terrain. In grabby crud you can step the front ski across the hill to "feel" the snow, then check your speed with the rear one. The step telemark is less strenuous than the full-on jump turn and is useful for a wider variety of conditions. It is also easier on us old guys.

Earlier in the advanced section I emphasized simultaneous movements from turn to turn: edging and weighting your skis at the same time to turn them smoothly as one. That kind of tele is the best way to achieve the smoothest arc with the least amount of skidding. But in certain situations it isn't necessarily a regression to choose sequential step-turning techniques rather than simultaneous ones. Sometimes you have to skid your skis in order to turn more

quickly. These are spots where, if you spend too much time carving through the fall line, you will pick up uncontrollable speed.

Step telemarks are a quicker, more advanced version of the half-wedge telemark. Pick a gentle, consolidated slope and push off into the fall line. Move from a straight parallel run into a telemark by *stepping* your front ski forward in a stem. That's right, step the front ski not only into the lead but with the ski stemmed, steering it into a new turn. You will need to emphasize the *forward* in this step so that the front ski doesn't cross the rear ski.

When stepping the front ski in a stem across the hill you will be into your turn quickly. Brace your weight against the edge of the front ski and step the rear ski alongside it, edging the snow hard. "Sting" the snow with the rear ski as you put it down. I like to count to myself: one (front step) two (rear step), and so on.

Now add a pole plant, stinging the snow with your downhill pole as you

Step telemarks: think one, two, one, two . . .

sting the snow with edge of the rear ski. I think one, sting, one, sting: one (front step), sting (rear step and pole plant), one, sting, one, sting. Practice it on the flats at slow speeds. It feels like you are "walking" down the hill, checking your speed with each ski/edge sting. With a little practice you can walk down anything: steeps, bumps, catchy crud. Remember, the rear ski controls your speed, so edge it fast and hard with your little toe when you step it around.

It's not the most elegant technique, but the step telemark is a godsend for controlling your speed in hairy situations. The more tools like jump turns and step teles that you learn the more fun you'll have when the skiing's not perfect.

TELEMARK CHRISTIES

Telemarks are indispensable in cruddy snow, very deep powder, crust, or any condition that yanks your feet back as momentum drags your body forward.

But parallel turns are much more secure on hard and refrozen snow, when falling forward is less likely but side-to side stability is elusive. There's a hybrid turn that combines the advantages of both: the telemark christy. The turn begins with a telemark and using an early lead change, finishes with a parallel.

Why a hybrid? Because starting a turn can be insecure with free-heel parallels. It's much more comfortable to initiate with a telemark and lead with one ski as a defense against forward falls. But at the end of the turn that leading foot is a handicap. To maintain the lead, your body rotates as your skis come across the hill—a very insecure attitude on steeps. Here, a parallel turn finish is more secure. The telemark christy combines the two turns, incorporating the stable turn initiation of the tele with the solid turn finish of a parallel.

Back to your practice slope. Warm up with some of your "classic" teles. In this maneuver your lead is changed be-

Lighten the uphill ski and
slide it forward

tween turns, just as you finish one and start the next. It's as though you are walking from turn to turn. The skis are across the fall line when you change leads.

Next try changing the lead earlier. Start the first turn with a telemark, standing tall and steering your skis into the fall line. As your skis find the fall line lighten the rear ski and slide it forward—I think of sliding it *through*. Your weight should shift to the outside ski for a secure parallel turn finish. The uphill ski, sliding forward, stays light and finishes the turn across the hill, slightly advanced in a parallel christy.

The sensation is as though you are "collecting" your skis and knees as your skis come out of the fall line. Some skiers think of it as lightening the uphill ski and sliding it forward. Or you may prefer to think of it as *driving your rear thigh forward* into an Alpine stance.

However you choose to think of it, notice in the sequence of illustrations how the telemark lead disappears and the turn is finished with most of the weight on the outside ski, Alpine style. You check your speed facing downhill in anticipation of the next turn. Using the slightly advanced uphill ski of the parallel turn, you have the proper lead to smoothly and quickly initiate a new telemark. There's no need for a strenuous lead change in that split second between turns. With practice you will find this earlier lead transition much smoother and quicker than changing your lead between turns. It's not meant to replace the smooth, classic "cruising" telemark but rather to add another turn variation to your repertoire.

CRUD

A few springs ago a whole pack of us were skiing in the Upper Kern Basin in California's Eastern Sierra. We made a base camp after the long approach into the basin, venturing out on day trips from there. We'd cut up a slope wherever we found good snow and cut up some spots where it wasn't so good. The last day we took an especially long tour to take a look at part of the Sierra's "Red Line Traverse." When we spotted a nearby peak with a beautiful slope we decided to take a break for some turns. From a distance, it looked to be a wonderful couloir to ski: steep, well-covered, and not too narrow. But as we climbed up the gully it was obvious that turning was going to be difficult. There was no bottom to the snow, just deep crud with a slightly frozen crust.

We reached a high point in the couloir where it took a dog leg and decided that was high enough. I took off my skins and tested the snow in a traverse. It was soft underneath, seemingly bottomless, yet topped with a weird frozen crust. It yanked at my feet as I tried to turn. The only turn that might work, it seemed, was a last resort: the jump turn. Some call it the survival or gorilla turn. I call it "hop and hope": jump up, twist your skis 180 degrees in the air, and land prepared for another jump. There's nothing fluid about it. Jump turns are jerky and tiring, but they work.

Like a bunch of uncoordinated grasshoppers we hopped our way down the slope one at a time, swapping teles and parallels at random. Our butts served as emergency brakes when the going got too fast. We all fancied ourselves confirmed crud skiers yet felt lucky to reach the bottom with our knees intact. No one volunteered to climb back up and do it again. Sure, it was "interesting" snow, but once was enough.

HOP AND HOPE

Most skiers avoid difficult snow. It hurts their knees and their egos. And then there are some like a Swiss friend

of mine who claims "there is no bad snow, just bad skiers." Bull. There is plenty of bad snow. But just because it's bad, just because it's difficult, doesn't mean it's not skiable. "Survival" skiing can provide some of the most rewarding turning there is.

In soft crud I keep my skis *in* the snow as much as possible and ski it like powder, using an exaggerated flexion and extension of my legs. Terrain allowing, I'll use larger-radius turns—speed helps you plow through heavy snow.

When the snow is desperate, though, I choose to leap and land (hop and hope). What's desperate? Set-up crud, breakable crust, snow that is just too unpredictable or too dangerous to push through. In those situations, especially with free heels, you are wise to get out of the snow and into the air. I find the "collected" position of the parallel turn the most effective for leaping and landing.

Jump turns combine several deliberate, consecutive movements into one athletic change of direction. In other words they're hard to do and hard to describe. They are easier to mimic by watching a good skier hop down the hill. Here's the sequence: (1) traverse to gain speed with skis parallel; (2) anticipate the upcoming turn, facing *directly* down the fall line; (3) set your uphill edges to make a platform and plant your pole down the hill; (4) grunt out loud, pushing up hard off of the platform and sharply raising your outside arm; (5) suck up your legs, cranking your skis around; and (6) land with your skis parallel and traverse to the next spot where you want to turn.

Don't worry if you didn't get all of that because I'll go over it again. Note that to practice jump turns you should thoroughly understand the chapter on "Skiing from the Waist Up." You will need many of the same ideas—skiing tough conditions are where clean technique and good body position really count. Difficult snow is like a magnifier. It emphasizes each unnecessary little quirk in your technique and uses each one against you. You must go back to the basics: shoulders faced down the hill, hands held ahead, pole plants properly timed, and skillful edging.

On the slope it's easiest to practice crud turns one at a time. As long as you have the room you can make one turn, regain your composure in a traverse, then make another turn. When making one turn at a time, however, you can't use the energy stored from the finish of the last turn to snap you into the next. Here you'll need a "pre turn" to set you up for each complete turn: you need to execute a strong, sinking-and-edging motion before you push off into the new turn—numbers one, two, and three above make up this "pre-turn."

Okay, we're on the slope. Get a bit of speed up and then sink quickly, planting your pole as you edge and weight both skis. That's your pre-turn.

Now, step four: extend your legs and stand up abruptly. Push off that plat-form with *both* feet and launch your body into the air. Raise your outside arm sharply to help give yourself more lift. You can see that move in the second figure of the parallel-jump-turn illustration.

Think of your legs as landing gear. As your skis lighten toward the end of your body's upward extension lengthen your air time by "bringing up the landing gear." Suck up your legs and bring them out of the snow. With your legs contracted and skis pulled upward, you are now free of whatever catchy snow you are trying to avoid. Point your skis in the desired direction and make your turn in midair—step five.

Once your skis are turned lower your landing gear and finish your turn. Reach for the snow with your legs extended so you can absorb the shock as you land—step six. Landing and absorbing with *both* of your legs will store energy for your next leap.

To execute jump turns you must use a strong pole plant. If you plant your pole in the right *place* at the right *time*,

A parallel jump turn

the wound up energy in your abdomen and torso will do most of the turning for you. Sound familiar? You must be very anticipatory and totally committed to each upcoming turn, facing directly down the fall line. Plant your pole in the fall line directly below your boots — clear back by your heel if it's steep — not forward toward your tips. This pole plant position forces your torso to face down the hill and increases the "wind-up" effect. Note the strong pole plants of the first and last figures in the illustration.

The pole plant is a firm, decisive *sting* that punctuates the end of each turn and the start of the next. Brace your torso with the pole. Your torso will want to rotate through the turn finish, but poling stops this movement and stores the energy in the muscles of your back and abdomen. As you leap up and bring your skis out of the snow, this stored muscular energy launches your skis into the next turn.

TELEMARK JUMP TURNS

In many situations I use jump parallel turns. But if advanced parallel turns aren't in your bag of tricks yet, or if you prefer telemarks, you will want to practice jump-tele turns. If you are a parallel skier tele turns will be fun to do for a change. The timing, pole plant, and anticipatory moves of teles are the same as in parallel turns.

The big difference that I find between jump teles and jump parallels is in getting my hips around from one tele to the next while in midair. It takes a lot of *punch*. In some snow I prefer using the telemark christy with an early lead change so that I can make the pre-turn in a stable parallel position. Plus, when finishing in a parallel turn you already have the correct lead for initiating the next tele.

Here's the sequence using the classic telemark lead change: (1) traverse in a telemark position, downhill foot advanced; (2) sink and edge—big-toe, little-toe—to make a pre-turn, anticipating with your torso and planting your pole firmly; (3) push up hard off the balls of both feet and "walk" forward, changing leads into a new tele as your skis lighten from your sharp upward movement (it will help with teles, too, to raise your outside arm sharply); (4)

A telemark jump turn

suck up your "landing gear" and turn your airborne skis; and (5) land in the next tele, ready for your traverse and another turn.

You can also use an earlier lead change in jump teles, which is my preference. The chief difference is in the traverse-and-turn initiation: (1) you make the initial traverse in a *parallel position*; (2) when you sink and edge for your pre-turn, it's in a parallel turn rather than a tele (face down the fall line as you pre-turn, planting your pole in anticipation of the upcoming turn into the fall line); (3) push off as in a parallel jump turn, raising your outside arm; (4) once your body is tall, suck your legs up and turn your skis, landing in a tele; and (5) tele turn out of the fall line, quickly sliding the uphill ski forward into a parallel position for your next parallel pre-turn.

It's optimistic to think that you can jump right into difficult snow and practice linked short turns. First practice the proper techniques in an easier situation, not necessarily on groomed conditions but in a better exposure, one

with less wind deposition and that's not so steep. Learn the sensations in this environment. When you jump into harder snow imagine yourself making and feeling the same moves as you did in practice.

Practice the turns one at a time as I have described them. This makes the fall line less intimidating. As your confidence grows try eliminating the traverse altogether. Jump from one turn to another with a "fall line attitude." It is strenuous, but when you get the hang of it you will be able to use the snap in your skis to take much of the effort out of your jump.

Easy to say, I know. With practice, you really will find turns of this kind quite easy. Learn the timing, visualize it in your mind's eye, and ski the image that you "see."

MOGULS

For years I refused to ski bumps at the resorts. I would go to great lengths to avoid mogul slopes, ricocheting across desperate traverses in search of groomed or windswept terrain. I rationalized that I was a cruiser. The fact was, I wasn't very comfortable in bumps, so I avoided them.

Although it's easy to visualize skiing the steep and deep, I wasn't really good at it back then, especially if it wasn't champagne powder. It wasn't until I learned to ski moguls that the steep and deep got easier. Once armed with better mogul technique, those steep shots in the trees became less intimidating to me. Fall line turns became the norm. They were easier to make exactly where I needed to turn. Because I no longer avoided moguls, my favorite ski areas grew into acres of new terrain.

You don't need to make lightning tele-lead switches and desperate recoveries to be a good mogul skier. Or to suffer knee-pounding turns when ricocheting off each mogul. There are points of focus that will help you become a smooth, controlled mogul skier who arrives at the bottom, run after run, with limbs and equipment intact. Many of these moves are the same ones you've focused on all along in your free-heel skiing. They are the same skills looked at in a slightly bumpier perspective.

It's most important to make up your mind that moguls aren't the enemy. Gritting your teeth while aggressively slamming each bump won't make them go away. Yeah, people do it under the lifts run after run. They probably have young knees. Skis bend, buckles break, bindings rip out, headaches throb. Stay light and relaxed and flow with the hill and gravity. Don't fight them. Aggressive skiing doesn't just mean "heavy and hard," it also means light and quick.

Something that contributes to that light, quick feeling is rhythm. Visit a resort like Telluride or Taos and you'll find many good bump runs—and little else to ski. No doubt there's lots of

Craig Hesse in the fall line
Photo by Ace Kvale

other terrain, but the long, unbroken steep slopes that characterize these areas are usually well-endowed with moguls. They may look frightening at first, but remember that these noteworthy resorts have bumps shaped by expert skiers on long skis. With a relaxed attitude and a little practice you'll find lines through these moguls that are steep but reasonable. Bumps carved with rhythm provide that incredibly exhilirating feeling of weightlessness between turns that is caused by flowing with the pull of gravity.

Odd as it sounds, it helps to develop a rhythm for mogul skiing by practicing *out* of the bumps on a smooth, moderately steep slope. Make a series of short-radius turns, confining them to a narrow imaginary "corridor" down the fall line. Or better yet, find a single-width snow cat track that goes directly downhill and use it for your corridor. If you finish each turn to control your speed you will soon feel the rhythm you're after. If your rhythm feels jerky and syncopated, try concentrating on facing down the hill even more than you ever have before.

How do you face your body down the hill *more*?

A skier refines his movements in increments. "Facing the fall line" is not the same for a skier working on beginning wedge turns as it is for a skier making advanced parallel turns. Facing the fall line is crucial in moguls. Look down the hill and feel that light, free separation of your upper and lower body. Your torso should "float" down the hill while your skis snap rhythmically back and forth to control your speed.

TIPS FOR THE TROUGHS

Most skiers agree it's easiest to begin your mogul skiing in the troughs. Look for a moderate-angled mogul slope with small, well-spaced bumps. On slopes that are occasionally groomed the bumps don't grow too large. Choose a "corridor" like the one you used on the smooth slope. Look ahead down the corridor (your "line") and make those same round, controlled turns in the smooth spots between the moguls. Keep your eyes several bumps ahead and avoid looking down at your tips.

POINTS OF FOCUS

Try thinking shoulders. Face them down the hill. It may help to hold your downhill shoulder back as you plant your pole. This will twist your torso so it faces the fall line, preparing it for the upcoming turn.

If you lean or bank in your turns you might have difficulty getting your skis around. This is a problem common among telemarkers. The symptoms are similar to not facing the fall line: you have good longer turns, but you have difficulty with the short fall-line turns required for moguls. An elegant technique in deep snow, banking will only get you into trouble in the bumps.

To avoid banking, ski with your abdomen. Point your belly button directly down the hill. Review the string-in-the-navel idea. Feel the muscles on the uphill side of your abdomen stretch, the ones on the downhill side contract. Go back to the pencil trick and pinch an imaginary pencil between your hip bone and abdominal muscles. Feel your abdominals doing more of the work.

Moguls can wreak havoc with a skier's hand position. Uphill hands that persistently drop behind twist the body into the hill and set you up for a nasty

fall. Try *especially* hard to keep your hands down the hill and within your peripheral vision. It helps to think of forcing your uphill hand downhill. It's like punching a bag. Push your uphill hand ahead of the downhill one that's planting the pole.

What about your feet? Converging or diverging skis can be deadly in a sea of bumps. You've got to edge both skis — tele or parallel — to keep them travelling in the same direction. Change your focus from hands to feet, edging both skis simultaneously. Think about your inside (rear for tele skiers) knee — point it in the direction of each new turn. Alpine skiers actually lead with it.

As you watch good mogul skiers you will notice the aggressive, determined pole plant that signals each new turn. In short-radius turns through bumps, plant your pole at the finish of each turn to coincide with the "sting" of your edges as you check your speed and set up for the next turn.

As important as *when* you plant your pole is *how* and *where*. Plant the basket down the hill beneath your downhill foot so that your body is "open" to the upcoming turn. Reach downhill — not toward your tips. With your skis across the hill, your basket should be back by your heel as you set up for a short-radius turn.

GETTING OUT OF THE TROUGHS

An Alpine instructor once showed me a trick called "log walking." It works great with either tele or parallel turns. You simply step over the mogul. I know. Looking down Tourist Trap at Vail, the idea of stepping over chest-high bumps seems improbable. Trust me. As your ski tips are pushed up by a mogul, step over the top of it with your uphill ski as though the mogul were a log. In a parallel turn step onto your new outside ski and steer it into the fall line. In a telemark step *forward* onto your new outside, leading ski, steering

Teles in moguls

a new telemark into the fall line. Try it. As your skis ride up the bump quickly step over the top. Exaggerate the movement and you will be log hopping instead of log walking.

It might take more than blithe hopping to get over the tops of huge moguls. You will need more shock absorption with another focus: your knees. I think of "lifting" my knees to absorb an especially large bump. I don't want to wait stiff-legged until the bump shoves my knees up into my chest. It's as though you anticipate each bump in or-

der to soften the blow. Time it right, lift your knees, and you can log walk over even huge bumps.

STANDING UP

Find a skier on the hill who stays low in the bumps. You won't have to look for long because getting low in bumpy situations is a natural reaction. Chances are the skier you're watching will do okay in the first few turns. But he'll soon start getting thrown around and compressed lower and lower until

he has nowhere to go. With no more shock absorption he becomes a human projectile ricocheting off each undulation in the terrain. Stuck in the back seat, he's lost his shock absorption by over-compressing his springs—his legs. By extending your legs between turns and standing tall, you can stretch those springs to prepare for another compression.

That's the other half of that leg-lifting business: extending your legs. Log walking helps because there's a natural extension when you step over something. But if you feel as though you are getting smaller and smaller as you pound down the hill, try standing up taller as you *press your skis* into the valley before the next bump. If you are turning in the valleys the motion will be the same as in skiing deep snow, when you press your skis into a new turn as you drop off your platform. You can use this technique with either teles or parallels. Your legs will feel like pneumatic shock absorbers, rythmically expanding and contracting to the beat of the bumps.

When using parallels, rise over the mogul, press on the balls of your feet, and press your tips down into the trough. In a telemark, emphasize the front ski, pressing the tip the same way into the trough. Press on the front foot, then finish the turn and control your speed with the rear ski.

Each day you venture into the bumps you will find yourself more in tune with your body's position and less intimidated by surprises. You will begin to venture into the bumps purposefully—or at least not go out of your way to avoid them. Your favorite ski area will get bigger. So will your options. Most important, all of your skiing will improve—even on the steep and deep!

AZU

I lived in Canada one winter in the 1970s. There wasn't much snow in the Canadian Rockies that year, so my partner and I explored other Canadian ranges that had gotten big dumps. We were both into track skiing as well as backcountry and tele-mark, so we had several kinds of skiing to choose from—whichever looked the best.

One of the places I wanted to explore was the Cariboo Region. I liked the name. Located between the Coast Range and the Rockies in the center of British Columbia, the Cariboo Region was rumored to be having a good winter. Our first destination was near 110 Mile House, a working ranch with about a hundred kilometers of prepared tracks. We packed up the car with an assortment of skis and made a beeline north from our base in the southern end of the province.

The skiing turned out to be fantastic. We spent a week at the ranch, kicking and gliding to our hearts' content in superb conditions. But my feet were getting sore from the cold and so many kilometers in the hard, well-groomed tracks. I met a wonderful couple who were obviously pine-cone-eaters out for a change of pace, kicking and sticking along with heavy wool knickers, day packs, and sixty-five milli-meter skis. They lived in Prince George, a pulp mill town on the Nacheko River—pretty far north. The

Facing down the hill
Photo by Michael Kennedy

165

skiing up there? It was a cold, snowy winter. The local trails were in excellent shape. And there was some really incredible powder skiing—about three hours farther north of Prince George, at a little Alpine resort called Azu.

I had always liked names like Prince George and Prince Rupert and Sir Donald and Sir Sanford. Those names conjure images of wild country, big country, endless northern expanses and high Alpine peaks. Restless for a new area, we packed and headed north.

Yes, Prince George, seven hours north from 110 Mile House, *was* having a heavy winter. And yes, it was cold. The first day we skied at Tabor Mountain, a local Nordic area that boasted exciting terrain with prepared tracks, skied-in trails, tourers' huts, and fantastic views of the north beyond. Special Green was the wax of the day, just like in Colorado.

The next day, unlike in Colorado, it rained. The temperature had risen fifty or sixty degrees overnight, and our Special Green fluff had turned to Special Red muck. I racked my brain for a place to go that might have good snow. What was the name of that little place? Azu? Again we headed north.

Any of you who have counted mileposts in the north country would recognize the scenic drive: prefab homes with a couple of trucks and a customized car, mangy dogs, the occasional BAR and EAT and

MOTEL. And distance. I love that distance, the sunsets, the stunted black spruce.

It was getting very snowy. We were approaching Pine Pass at the northern end of the Rocky Mountain Trench, the "valley" between the Rockies and the Interior Range. The snow looked wonderful. "Who needs a ski area?" we said. "Let's just find a turnaround, park, and slap on our skins. The snow looks perfect everywhere."

But the next turnaround was Azu. It's located on the provincial highway about an hour south of Fort Saint John, the start of the Alaska Highway. A DMC Thiokol was plowing its tiny little parking lot. There was a pre-fab trailer-like building that said EAT, and some low shed-like buildings labeled MOTEL. Where was BAR? Above rose Azu—a short but steep slope, ungroomed, and a short t-bar.

The mountain manager met us in the parking lot. "We don't do much groomin' here, but this Thiokol is sure handy for plowin' the parking lot, eh? Too late? No, it's best you didn't get here any sooner; we didn't get five skiers until eleven A.M., and we won't open with less than five, eh? How much new snow? Oh, not so much, about forty to fifty centimeters. We've been gettin' that 'most every day, eh? I think the base is about five meters. We need it to cover the willows, eh? Lift ticket? Don't worry about it, go ski and I'll get you at the end of the day. Tell my brother at the lift you talked to me. And at the end of the day—if you'd like—you can ski off the top of the lift toward that open, untracked slope you passed down the highway. Remind me and I'll come get you in the truck. Have a good day, eh?"

Azu claims sixty-five feet of accumulated snowfall per season—more than any other North American ski area. Back then they had an application in for a government grant. They had big plans: chair lifts, helicopters, restaurants, and hotels. The only problem was people: there just weren't that many local skiers in Chetwind and Fort Saint Jimmy.

I was shaking. I couldn't get suited up fast enough. We introduced ourselves to John's brother, who was running the little t-bar. How long is the lift? Twelve hundred feet—that's all the cable they had when they built it.

The skiing brought tears to my eyes. It was one of the rare times I've felt that sensation of dropping through baseless powder on my tele skis. Floating, turn after turn.

On our skinny skis we were the talk of the town. We were the first telemarkers they had seen. Everybody came out to ski with us: the ski school director (and sole instructor), the mountain manager (mechanic and Thiokol operator), the lift operator (and fry cook at EAT). We had a wonderful time. We had planned to stay a couple of days but we stayed a week. It snowed at least eighteen inches each night.

The Azu area got that government grant it wanted and expanded. My buddies in Prince George tell me that I wouldn't recognize it anymore. I don't think I'll go back. The memory of that first experience is too good. And there must be another Azu somewhere.

BIBLIOGRAPHY

Abraham, Horst. *Skiing Right*. Boulder, Colorado: Johnson Books, 1983

Hall, Bill. *Cross Country Skiing Right*. San Francisco: Harper and Row, 1985.

Joubert, Georges. *Teaching Yourself to Ski*. Aspen, Colorado: Aspen Ski Masters, 1970.

Lunn, Arnold. *A History of Skiing*. Oxford: Oxford University Press, 1927.

Tejada-Flores, Lito. *Backcountry Skiing: The Sierra Club Guide to Skiing Off the Beaten Track*. San Francisco: Sierra Club Books, 1981.

Tejada-Flores, Lito. *Breakthrough on Skis: How to Get Out of the Intermediate Rut*. New York: Vintage Books, 1986.

INDEX

Free-Heel Skiing was designed by Daniel Earl Thaxton.
It was typeset in Goudy Old Style by Dartmouth Printing Company.
It was printed on Finch Opaque, an acid-free paper, by Bookcrafters.